Mission Tour

Bruce Fawcett • Mike McDonald • Rob Nylen

Mission Tour

SUCCESSFULLY LEADING YOUTH

ON A SHORT-TERM MISSION EXPERIENCE

CONVENTION of Atlantic Baptist Churches
CONVENTION des Églises Baptistes de l'Atlantique

The text was typeset in Aldus, Palantino & Scala Sans at Gaspereau Press. Cover design by Mark MacDonald of PinPoint Creative Group.

National Library of Canada Cataloguing in Publication

Fawcett, Bruce
Mission tour: successfully leading youth on a short-term mission experience / Bruce Fawcett, Mike McDonald, Rob Nylen.

Previously published under title: Youth mission tours.

ISBN 0-9688758-4-X

I. Youth in missionary work – Canada. I. McDonald, Mike (Michael William) II. Nylen, Rob, 1973– III. Convention of Atlantic Baptist Churches. IV. Fawcett, Bruce. Youth mission tours. V. Title.

BV2617.F39 2005 266'.00835'0971
C2005-901348-6

Published by:
THE CONVENTION OF ATLANTIC BAPTIST CHURCHES
1655 MANAWAGONISH ROAD
SAINT JOHN, NB, CANADA E2M 3Y2
PHONE: (506) 635-1922
FAX: (506) 635-0366
EMAIL: CABC@BAPTIST-ATLANTIC.CA

Dedicated to Rev. Dr. David R. Watt
Husband, father, pastor, mission strategist, visionary, mentor of young leaders and early leader of the youth mission tour movement in Atlantic Canada

Other Books Available from the Convention of Atlantic Baptist Churches

Youth Mission Tours (2001)
BY BRUCE FAWCETT AND MIKE MCDONALD

Effective Evangelism in Atlantic Canada (2001)
EDITED BY BRUCE FAWCETT, STEPHEN MCMULLIN, DAVID MOREHOUSE, AND KEVIN VINCENT

Effective Youth Ministry (2003)
EDITED BY BRUCE FAWCETT AND ROB NYLEN

Missional Youth Ministry (2004)
EDITED BY BRUCE FAWCETT AND ROB PATTERSON

To Order

THE CONVENTION OF ATLANTIC BAPTIST CHURCHES
1655 MANAWAGONISH ROAD
SAINT JOHN, NB, CANADA E2M 3Y2
PHONE: (506) 635-1922
FAX: (506) 635-0366
EMAIL: CABC@BAPTIST-ATLANTIC.CA

Contents

Preface & Acknowledgments

Over the years we have witnessed first hand the power of the mission tour movement as it has brought energy and focus to youth ministries across Atlantic Canada and beyond. Many university students, as they reflect back upon their youth group years, report that it was during a mission tour that they encountered God in a new and fresh way. Many students say that it was while doing mission that they were challenged to deepen their Christian commitment. A significant number of students say that they experienced a call to vocational ministry through summer mission experiences.

This book's purpose is to enable more youth groups to take advantage of this wonderful movement God is using in the lives of students. The suggestions we share in this book come from lessons God is teaching us. We believe this book will convince you that short-term mission should be an integral part of your church's youth ministry. It will also help you successfully integrate mission experiences to your youth ministry. May God bless you as you serve Him, His church, and His teens!

Significant portions of this book appeared previously as *Youth Mission Tours* published by the United Baptist Convention of the Atlantic Provinces (now known as the Convention of Atlantic Baptist Churches) in 2001. Portions of chapter 16 previously appeared in *Missional Youth Ministry* published by the Convention of Atlantic Baptist Churches in 2004.

We would like to express our appreciation to Gary Dunfield and Andrew Steeves of Gaspereau Press and Mark MacDonald of PinPoint Creative Group, for their encouragement, helpful suggestions, and timely service. We would also like to thank Dave Egers, Phil Harbridge, Marlene Knowles, Greg Pike, Dale Stairs, Mark Sypher and Phil Woodworth for their many helpful and insightful comments on the text.

Finally, to our wives and family, who supported us and encouraged us through this project we say, thank you and we love you very much!

BRUCE FAWCETT
MIKE MCDONALD
ROB NYLEN

Foreword

Dr. Harry Gardner

As Executive Minister I have been privileged to experience worship in a variety of places around the world. In the summer of 2004 I had the opportunity to travel to Seoul, Korea to take part in the meetings of the Baptist World Alliance Council. One experience I had while there was to be part of a prayer service in a local church. It was clearly unlike any worship service I had ever attended. On that occasion there were 22,000 people present for an all-night prayer meeting. They all prayed together at the same time, out loud! We could hear their prayers from outside the building as we approached the church and we were overwhelmed at the sense of God's presence.

Two days later I had the privilege to be back in Fredericton, New Brunswick, for an evening rally at Tidal Impact 2004. In that rally, I sensed the same movement of God, the same depth and power as the teens and leaders submitted their lives to the Lord through the participation in the Lord's Supper. The experience in Fredericton was every much as powerful as the prayer service in Korea. It was truly an amazing experience!

Mission tours have been an instrumental part of our shared ministry in Atlantic Canada. I am proud that we can boast of such a marvellous movement that has been a significant force not only in youth groups, but in local churches of our Convention and beyond. There is nothing like it across our country. I have seen the value of the mission tour in my home church, Grand Bay Baptist Church. I have enjoyed watching our own teens mature in their faith and grow as they serve others.

As I travel around our region, I have talked with many pastors who have valued the role of the mission tour movement in discipling their own youth. Others have also commented on its benefit to their ministry as teens came and served in their church. I have also enjoyed listening to many young pastors who are seeking accreditation in our Convention talk about how they have cut their teeth in ministry during mission tours. These mission tours are creating a generation of young leaders who understand that it is normal to build a ministry around mission and service.

I believe it is fair to say that Bruce, Mike and Rob know what they are talking about when it comes to planning and leading mission tours. If I were to add up the total number of mission tours these three have led, it would be close to forty. If I added up the number of teens they have personally led on mission tours, it would be over 1000. If I added up the number of teens who have attended mission tours these three have planned it would be over 10,000. In short, out of their experience comes a wisdom and practicality that will ensure a successful short-term mission experience for the youth of your church that benefits God's Kingdom.

Finally, what I appreciate about this resource is that it evolves from a passion to see teens experience mission. When Bruce, Mike and Rob were youth pastors they saw mission tours strengthen their own churches and now they want to ensure they continue to impact our region. Take this book and read it carefully. Pass it out to others who will be serving on your mission trips. May God bless you as you participate in the Kingdom work.

DR. HARRY GARDNER
Executive Minister
Convention of Atlantic Baptist Churches

1 Why Should I do a Mission Tour with my Youth Group?

Bruce Fawcett

Before we talk about the value of a mission tour to your youth ministry it is important to describe what is meant by the expression "mission tour." The phrase "mission tour" is unique to Atlantic Canada and is generally used to refer to two kinds of short-term youth mission projects. First, it refers to a large multi-church mission experience, such as Tidal Impact, where over one hundred mission teams descend upon a target area and cooperatively engage in ministries of evangelism and social concern. The nature of this type of project will be described in chapter five.

Secondly, "mission tour" also refers to any short-term experience undertaken by a youth mission team from a church or ministry. This kind of project could be done alone or in partnership with other churches. It could be ministry done in the inner-city, overseas, at a camp, or in partnership with a local church.

It takes a lot of work to take a group of teenagers on a mission tour. Between preparation for ministry, fundraising and being away from home during the trip itself, a mission tour is a major commitment for a church and it's youth leaders. Is it worth it? There are many reasons why a mission tour can contribute to making your youth ministry sharper and more effective:

Focuses your ministry on what's important: A mission tour is not simply a nice trip to tack on to the end of a ministry year. Involving your youth group in a mission tour can significantly alter and enhance the kind of youth ministry that takes place in your church.

When Darren McHarg was called to be the first full-time youth pastor at the Jacksonville Baptist Church outside of Woodstock, New Brunswick, the church already had a well-established youth ministry. They had a core of several dozen students who enjoyed their youth group and their leaders and looked forward to being together for their weekly meetings. The search committee, though, impressed upon Darren their desire to enhance their youth ministry by developing a service or mission component.

For Darren, the summer mission tour was the answer to the question of how to move his group on to their next stage of growth. Building on the foundation he already had, he encouraged his teenagers to sign up for the team he was taking to Bold and Alive '95, a large multi-church mission experience held in Moncton. He soon discovered that to get them ready he had to train them and help them prepare spiritually through a required discipleship component. The benefit of Bold and Alive was greater than the one week of mission; it forced him to add a training and discipling component to his ministry.

The number of students involved in the summer mission program at Jacksonville grew each year and the youth ministry of the church was enhanced as the program developed an increased emphasis on ministry training and discipleship.

A mission tour can provide a focus for leaders who want to move their ministry in the direction of discipleship, ministry training and involvement in mission. Since teenagers have to prepare to go on the mission trip, your church's youth program will naturally have to allow opportunities for training and spiritual preparation. Churches who make involvement in mission tour a "privilege" and not a "right" also have the opportunity to require such things as regular attendance at Bible study and worship, ministry involvement in the home church and a daily quiet time with God.

This sort of leadership development before you go on your trip allows teenagers to learn more about God and grow closer to him. It also allows teenagers to discover and use their spiritual gifts. It reminds them that ministry can and should occur at home as well as away. Acquiring this outward focus helps them discover that the church exists not primarily for those inside the walls but for those who have not yet come to know Christ.

Exposing young people to mission is key to creating mission-minded congregations. The mission tour movement is contributing to renewal and growth in churches across the Atlantic region and beyond.

Corrects the imbalance of 20th century evangelicalism: The evangelical Protestant movement in the 20th century had a lot of strengths, including a stress on the importance of orthodoxy, an emphasis on personal piety and a passion for evangelism. However, a key element that was often missing from the movement was recognition that social action has an important part to play in the ministry of the church.

It is time to bring wholeness to the gospel and correct this imbalance. In many churches significant steps have been taken, but across Atlantic Canada much work still needs to be done. Our gospel needs to be "full-orbed." That is, it needs to respond faithfully to Christ's command to "make disciples of all nations" (Matthew 28:19) and to "love your neighbor as yourself" (Matthew 22:39). A strong commitment to the importance and urgency of evangelism is vitally important both to the health of a church and to the spiritual vitality of individual believers. At the same time, individuals and churches must remember that exhibiting a concern for the physical wellbeing of people enhances our witness and follows the example of Christ. There are those who understand the love of Christ because they are told about it with words. There are many others who only understand the love of Christ because someone takes the time to show them through their actions.

The large multi-church mission experiences work hard to show students that it is important to tell people about Christ through words, but it is also important to show people the love of Christ through ministries of compassion. Students are given the opportunity on a mission tour to lead children to faith in Christ in a morning evangelistic program. In the afternoon, the same teenagers are invited to take part in a food drive so that the hungry in the host city will have a meal to eat next week. Christian teenagers need to experience a full-orbed gospel! All short-term mission trips should look to include both of these elements into their experience.

Helps teach teenagers the meaning for life: Emily Hastings was one of a large group of students from Kennebecasis Baptist Church in Quispamsis, New Brunswick who took part in Tidal Impact 2002. Later, as a university student, when she reflected back on her Tidal Impact experience, she says one of the chief lessons she learned was one of life's greatest ironies – that the more you give, the more you get. By this she means that she discovered that meaning and purpose for life comes from serving others. This is a very profound and fundamental truth about life. Unfortunately many people never discover this truth because it runs so counter to the messages about meaning found in popular culture.

There are many teenagers who have bought into the message of the culture around them that suggests that you will find happiness when you acquire more money, more possessions and more power. All of these things can bring happiness for a time, but once we reach our financial goal we find that we want more money. Once we acquire the possession we have desired we discover that the joy isn't all we thought it might be, so we strive for something "greater."

As youth leaders we do students a great disservice if we do not help them discover at an early age that ministry to others in Jesus' name can bring a rich sense of purpose and fulfillment.

The mission tour movement seeks to provide opportunities for students to minister in a variety of settings so that they can experience the joy that comes from serving others. If our churches are not helping teenagers in this critically important area of self-discovery then we are shortchanging them in a major area of human growth – the search for meaning.

Worship and teaching: When I've travelled to other areas of the globe and have had the opportunity to worship with believers from other cultures I've found it interesting but often not very fulfilling. One worship opportunity in a foreign language and culture is nice, but a steady diet of it is not all that rewarding! In the same way that I'm not sure I'd like to worship in someone else's culture regularly, teenagers tell me that a steady diet of worship in adult culture falls short of providing the kind of experience of God that they crave and desire. Human beings simply desire to worship God in their own culture and in their own language, and teenage human beings are no different from the rest of us. The worship style of most of our churches, though, is not geared to teenagers. So it is critically important for young people to understand that God can accept and appreciate worship in their language. As churches we may not be able to provide that opportunity every week, but we can provide alternate opportunities.

Worship is a key element of the mission tour movement. At combined events like Tidal Impact teenagers are given the opportunity to gather for collective worship. A worship team that understands how teenagers like to express their love and devotion for God helps create worship experiences that are rich and freeing, allowing them to experience God's presence in a new and fresh way.

These evening rallies also include dynamic teaching from God's word as well. Most young people who have ministered diligently all day are in need of encouragement and helpful instruction from God's word. This teaching fills the tank of those who have given out so much during the day.

If you are preparing your own short-term mission project, you should give high consideration to including a daily worship component, so students have the opportunity to respond to what they have witnessed God do during the day. You don't need the light show and big band of larger events. Often a guitar and a group of "filled up" teens can create powerful worship times.

Public witness: I can remember clearly during Tidal Impact 2004 being interviewed live in a radio studio in Fredericton, New Brunswick. I was asked why hundreds of students from across Canada would come to Fredericton and pay money to serve the community. The radio show's host expressed amazement that teenagers would pay money to come and work in a city they had never even visited before! I must confess, having been involved in the mission tour movement for years, I had simply forgotten how powerful a public witness such a project could be to the community at large.

A large multi-church mission tour is a powerful way to saturate a community. Hundreds of young Christian believers can make a huge impact upon a city! In events like Tidal Impact, thousands of children, teenagers and adults were exposed to the gospel. The result of working together is so much greater than what could be done apart. Frequently, the news media is eager to tell the story of the hundreds of teenagers who paid money to come and work in the local area.

The word on the street in Canada is that churches do not connect with the young in our society. This, of course, is simply not true. While there are challenges associated with transmitting the faith to the next generation in our country, it is also true that many churches have vibrant ministries to young people. A combined public effort demonstrates that many Canadian teenagers have a vibrant and energetic faith which is highly relevant to society's needs and very important to them personally. This is a powerful message to send to our secular society.

The impact on a local area can also be significant when a single team comes to an area and spends a large quantity of time building strong relationships. A smaller team can get to know the people, spend more time with them and can have a profound ministry impact. If a small team is travelling to an area, they may be wise to spend a more concentrated amount of time in one spot, instead of trying to hit multiple mission targets.

Fosters fellowship: Involvement in mission tours strengthens the bonds of fellowship in a variety of ways. First, training for a project and then carrying it out together will draw your youth group together. Both the experience itself and the shared reflection on the trip later will cause the friendship bonds within your group to be strengthened. Second, by meeting other believers from another church or ministry, students from your group will develop bonds with believers who they may meet at other youth events, attend university with, or meet up with when they move to a new community.

The linking of two churches together in ministry for a week also models for young people the power of partnership. Too many churches are going at it alone and are either unwilling or unable to work together. Teenagers need to see healthy and effective models of partnership and cooperation. If churches can't or won't work together their witness is needlessly hampered among the young who expect and demand such cooperation.

Holistic growth: A mission tour can be a significant growth experience for students. As they travel, students see the beauty of God's creation and learn more about the world they inhabit. Students also learn healthy travel skills like how to pace themselves and how to remain healthy on the road by getting the right amount of sleep and eating proper foods. Students also learn skills for getting along with one another. Most students have their own room at home so sharing a room with one or two others on a trip can stretch them in new ways. Mission tours also provide opportunity for romance to develop. What better place to meet one's future mate then on a mission project! Finally, immersion in a mission project also allows a student to explore a call to vocational ministry.

Adds energy to your summer ministry: In the summer of 1996 Gander Baptist Church in Gander, Newfoundland hosted a team from Hillside Baptist in Moncton, New Brunswick. Previously, the Gander church was only able to offer a one-day children's outreach program in the summer. With the arrival of the 12-member team from Moncton led by Pastor Darrell Bustin, the two churches partnered together and offered a full five-day Vacation Bible School program touching dozens of children in the city. Because of the partnership Gander's children's outreach was raised to a new, higher level.

Unlike Gander, there are some churches that run Vacation Bible School programs every summer. Sometimes though, having run the same type of program summer after summer, they feel that they could use an injection of energy and vigor to their summer outreach program. Churches frequently find that when teenagers are given the opportunity to lead they respond with excitement and dedication. The quality level of their program often rises even though the student leaders may be less experienced.

Similarly, many churches that are preparing to visit another church often decide to use the same curriculum for their own

Vacation Bible School program so that the teenagers can help out with the program at home before going away.

Either way, your summer ministry can benefit from a youth ministry program that emphasizes ministry training and involvement.

Appreciation of other ways of being the church: Mission tour involvement also exposes students to the breadth of worship and ministry styles within various churches. Perhaps the worship style in the church they are visiting is a little freer or more structured than they are used to at home. Perhaps they see church facilities that offer them a fresh perspective on their own. Perhaps they meet pastors who have a different approach to leadership and ministry then they have encountered before. All these things are part of growing up and recognizing the richness of the Christian movement in Canada.

Conclusion: Yes, a mission tour can be a fun experience, but it is so much more! By capitalizing on this movement of God, churches can strengthen and enhance the kinds of ministry they do with teenagers in their community, resulting in a much stronger and healthier church.

2 How To Integrate Mission Into Your Youth Ministry

Bruce Fawcett

Four students showed up for my first youth group meeting. The same four showed up for my second meeting and, yes, for my third meeting, the same four showed up. At least we had consistency going for us! As a new youth pastor at Lewisville Baptist Church in Moncton, New Brunswick, I quickly realized that we were not going to break youth group attendance records that summer or any time soon!

In those early months as a new youth pastor I began to feel that to justify my full-time salary, I was going to have to come up with a strategy to grow this group. As fall came, some students who had been away over the summer drifted back to our group and some of the pressure left my shoulders, but still the question remained: What would be our strategy for growing our youth ministry? The more I thought about the question over those early months of ministry I began to realize that while numerical growth was very important, designing a program that would also challenge teenagers to move to a higher level of faith commitment was even more important. After all, which is the greater mark of youth ministry success, a large youth group or youth who stay faithful to Christ through young adulthood? Long-term staying power was what I hoped for, prayed for and began to plan toward.

Eventually, through a combination of prayer and noticing the positive response of teenagers to mission projects, I concluded that the mission tour would be a very important part of our strategy for growing our group numerically and especially spiritually. For our church, the mission tour was not just a "nice trip" tacked on to our ministry year. It was the cornerstone of a strategic plan to grow our ministry, something we encouraged our students to work toward but also something we designed our program to lead toward. I have seen this approach work in many churches and it can in your church as well! To understand how the mission tour can serve as a critical component of a youth ministry growth strategy, let's examine the pyramid below.

The pyramid: The thought behind the youth ministry pyramid is that each youth ministry needs to offer programming at increasingly challenging levels in order to encourage teenagers to grow in their faith. If a youth program only runs fun events every week, then one should never expect that teenagers will grow to understand that daily scripture reading and sharing their faith are important. Not all of these levels of programming need to run concurrently. Most of these programs do not need to be offered weekly. What is more important, however, is that leaders have a plan to offer all of these levels of programming over the course of a year so that your church's youth ministry is well-balanced and encourages teenagers to grow in their commitment to Christ.

Target population: How many teenagers in your neighborhood or town speak the same language you speak in your ministry and do not attend another youth ministry? This group is your ministry target group. As a youth leader you are your church's leader of ministry to adolescents in your community. Therefore, you should know basic facts about your community such as how many teenagers live in your area and approximately how many of them attend other youth ministries. The Convention of Atlantic Baptist Churches has access to PCensus, a software program from Statistics Canada that will provide you with the demographic breakdown of your community, including the number of teenagers and many important facts about your ministry target area.

Come: Some of the teenagers in your target group will not come to an event your church sponsors. Maybe their parents will not allow them to go or perhaps they had a bad experience with a church at some point in their past. However, many students will come to a special event that your church hosts. To move people from the "target population" to the "come" level, your church should have an outreach event two to four times a year in order to reach these students and to provide a doorway they can pass through to become a regular part of your ministry. Christian teenagers in your church should help plan the special event and during the planning process they should be clearly taught what your ministry hopes to achieve by hosting this outreach event. During the event adults should do most of the work to allow your youth group members to spend time building relationships with their guests. Your event could be a concert, an all-night party, a day trip out of town, a paintball challenge, or anything else you dream up. What is popular in your community? What kind of event will excite students in your youth group and the community?

Many groups feel that they need to have an outreach event every week. Early on in a youth ministry it may be useful to have weekly fun events to build a sense of group identity and to build relationships between leaders and students. Over time though, it is generally a poor use of time and resources to have a program every week where students are invited to the church just to have fun.

The church is not the YMCA or the Boys and Girls Club. We have a different calling. The church exists to see people won to Christ and discipled in their faith. Generally, in a mature local church youth ministry, fun ought to be a bi-product of an event designed for spiritual purposes, not an end in and of itself.

Explore: When a guest attends an outreach event at your church you want to make sure that the visitor knows that he or she is invited to become a regular part of your ministry. Both a public and a personal invitation should be issued to the visitor at the outreach event, inviting him or her to return next week to your weekly youth meeting. In addition, you should also use mail and a follow-up phone contact to reiterate the invitation during the week following the outreach event. An outreach event that is planned without an effective strategy for follow up can be very frustrating for leaders and students alike. The absence of a follow-up plan virtually guarantees that all the work you put into planning the event will not achieve its desired end of connecting with new people and folding them into your ministry.

The program you should invite your visitors to return to is your weekly Bible study. This program, which may be held during the week or on the weekend, is designed to help people become disciples of Jesus. It should be broad enough in design that it both strengthens believers in their faith and also introduces seekers to the basics of the Christian faith. These Bible study groups, ideally, should not be larger than 8–12 students to allow for freedom of discussion and for a sense of community to develop. Dividing groups by age can be an advantage as well since high school students and middle school or junior high students think differently and are wondering about different issues. These groups can meet in homes or at the church building if facilities permit. Topics you may wish to cover include: Who is Jesus? What does the Bible have to say about dating? How can I understand my Bible? Did Jesus really rise from the dead? You may wish to have a sports or games time following your Bible study or even an opportunity for just hanging out. Larger groups frequently add a worship dimension to their Bible study program by having students or leaders lead a contemporary worship experience.

Many churches add a second dimension to the "explore" level by providing an opportunity for students to discover more about God on their own through an organized devotional or "Quiet Time" emphasis. Students are taught the importance of a daily devotional encounter with God and techniques for maintaining one's devotional life either during the Bible study program or at a special seminar. The youth leader then provides the interested students with the necessary resources such as a Bible in an understandable translation and a devotional guide. Sometimes churches also provide students with an adult mentor. This mentor meets with the student regularly to help him or her with problems and questions and so that they can hold each other mutually accountable in their commitment to maintaining regular devotional practices. To learn more about this see chapter seven.

Ministry training: Over time it will become clear that there are some students in your weekly Bible study group who are ready for a higher level of commitment and challenge. You should invite these students to become involved in a ministry training program. For some groups it will be best to run ministry training concurrently with your Bible study, either on the same evening immediately before or after your Bible study or on another evening during the week. For other churches it will be best to run this program consecutively. For instance, you can wrap up your Bible study program in late March or early April and offer a ministry training program for the remaining weeks of the academic year.

In different churches ministry training takes different forms. For some, it may mean forming a youth choir that will have the opportunity to sing in your church's worship services and also at events in nursing homes, hospitals or other venues. Some churches invest in a puppet ministry. Other churches train their teenagers to minister using drama, mime, or liturgical dance. The possibilities are limited only by your imagination! The bottom line, though, is to assist teenagers in their spiritual growth by helping them understand that once they have committed their lives to Christ and are growing in their faith they have the responsibility to share their ministry abilities and gifts with others. The Christian faith is not meant to be an armchair existence. All believers need to be taught to use the ministry gifts God has given them in order to build up the church and minister to a hurting world.

Mission: Many students who receive training in ministry and have an opportunity to discover and use their ministry gifts find that ministry is very rewarding and exciting. Many students will want to take their ministry talents and skills beyond their own town or city to serve Christ in other locales when given the opportunity. This is where the mission tour comes into your strategic plan. You should invite students who have gone through your Bible study and ministry training process to participate in a mission project.

There will be those in your youth ministry who will hear about your trip and will want to short-circuit the process by going on the trip without the necessary preparation. This approach of taking teenagers on a mission trip without preparation does not work to the advantage of the student, your youth group, or your partner church. If a student is asked to perform ministry tasks on a mission trip for which he or she has not been trained, the student will have a poor experience with ministry, which is the opposite of what the youth leader would hope. Similarly, someone who has not been properly trained may not be able to carry out all of their responsibilities. It is also unfair to a host church if you show up for a week of ministry with teenagers who are not prepared to perform the tasks that need to be done. Involvement in the training process must be required for all mission tour participants.

It has been my experience that for properly trained teenagers, a well-planned mission trip can be the highlight of their year. They will use their gifts, watch others grow, be challenged in their faith, build relationships with new friends, forge closer bonds with those in their own youth group and develop a closer relationship with God. Teenagers who have this kind of experience will likely come home excited and encourage others to take part in the training process so that they can go the next year.

Peer-to-Peer ministry: Some students who mature as a result of the mission tour experience will develop a burden for their friends. A successful ministry experience away from home can often serve to highlight the fact that their friends at home need counsel, support, prayer and a personal relationship with Jesus. Peer-to-peer ministry is placed at the top of the pyramid because it is the hardest type of ministry for an adolescent to engage in. It is easier to minister away from home than it is on one's home turf. It is easier to minister in a church building than it is outside. It is easier to minister to children than it is to one's peers. However, it is also true that the most lasting successful ministry occurs between friends. Churches can support this kind of ministry by hosting or taking students to special seminars designed to encourage such ministry as the middle school Quest conference.

Conclusion: This pyramid model is a strategy that allows us to point our ministry toward long-term success. Some groups are excited if they have one outreach event and attract 100 teenagers. Several dozen visitors could be a great response for another church. However, the real measure of success is how many of those visitors are folded into the church's weekly Bible study program, come to faith, become discipled and then remain true to their professed faith. If a big crowd was generated at a special event but the vast majority of attendees are never seen again, then the outreach event was not as successful as it first appeared.

The purpose of understanding youth ministry through the pyramid model is to help leaders recall that the goal is to see the number of teenagers involved in each ministry level grow a little each year. If you had 12 students at the "come" level last year, what could you do this year to bump that number up to 16? If your average Bible Study attendance last year was 25 students, what could you do this year to increase it to 28? In some situations growth is not possible due to factors beyond our control such as key families moving away from the community. However, in most communities in most years, growth should be our goal for we are about Kingdom work. We have a message, which, if accepted by individuals, can bring healing to families, personal peace, life direction and eternal salvation. We do not desire growth for growth's sake. We long to see our youth ministries connect with more people because every statistic represents someone whose life would be better if they had an intimate relationship with Jesus Christ.

As an integral component of a healthy youth ministry, a mission tour can play a key role in bringing about both numerical growth for your group and spiritual growth among those entrusted to your care.

3 Toward a Theology of Short-Term Mission

Mike McDonald

¶ Why consider short-term mission?

We all have reasons for the things we do. Sometimes our reasons are subconscious and other times we are very conscious of the things we promote or choose to do. Why should your youth group participate in a short-term mission experience? The teens in your group, their parents and the leadership of your church will invariably ask this question. Quite simply, you go on a mission tour to:

1. Do ministry
2. Be ministered to
3. Have fun

Veteran mission tour leaders know that students will often remember these reasons in the reverse order as the word "fun" may initially interest them the most. However, most participants discover after completing a mission project that the first two reasons grow in importance. Let's look at the biblical basis for these three underlying reasons behind a short-term mission project and why a mission tour is important to your youth ministry.

Scriptural basis: In his book, *Purpose Driven Youth Ministry*, veteran youth pastor Doug Fields looks at the Great Commandment and the Great Commission as providing the basic biblical foundation for youth ministry. He indicates that these two commands summarize all of the other passages in the New Testament and describe the five main purposes of the church and consequently, of a youth ministry.

> GREAT COMMANDMENT: *Jesus replied: "'Love the Lord your God with all your heart and with all your soul and with all your mind.' This is the first and greatest commandment. And the second is like it: 'Love your neighbour as yourself.' All the Law and the Prophets hang on these two commandments."*
>
> MATTHEW 22:37–40

> GREAT COMMISSION: *"Therefore go and make disciples of all nations, baptizing them in the name of the Father and of the Son and of the Holy Spirit, and teaching them to obey everything I have commanded you. And surely I am with you always, to the very end of the age."* MATTHEW 28:19–20

Fields then says that the five purposes are found in these two passages:

WORSHIP:	"Love the Lord your God with all your heart"
MINISTRY:	"Love your neighbour as yourself"
EVANGELISM:	"Go and make disciples"
FELLOWSHIP:	"Baptizing them"
DISCIPLESHIP:	"Teaching them to obey"

Fields (1998) goes on to state that these purposes drive his church and thousands of others. They are not new ideas, but have been handed down to us through scripture. You don't create these purposes you discover them. After reading *Purpose Driven Youth Ministry* I realized that the reasons I had been giving teens for going on mission tours reflected the five purposes Fields outlines from scripture.

MINISTRY EVANGELISM	1 – to do ministry
WORSHIP DISCIPLESHIP	2 – to be ministered to
FELLOWSHIP	3 – to have fun

These goals clearly reflect a biblical understanding of mission. We are called to be the people of God, to do His kingdom work, and in expressing the love of Christ others will see the joy of being a Christian. A mission tour will help us to accomplish these ministry goals as found in scripture. With this is mind, let's clarify some terms and then look in depth at each of our three reasons for mission tours.

¶ Defining ministry, service, evangelism & mission

In *The Purpose Driven Life* resources by Rick Warren, we encounter some excellent definitions that need to be considered before we look into the three categories that I have assembled. Warren helps distinguish between ministry and service in his sermon entitled "Shaped for Serving God."

> The only way you can serve God is by serving others. This is called "ministry," and it, like the other words, is a misunderstood word. Most people think of a priest or a pastor, but the Bible says every believer is a minister (not a pastor). Ministry simply means using my shape (**S**piritual gifts, **H**eart, **A**bilities, **P**ersonality, and **E**xperiences) to help somebody else in the name of God. That's called ministering, and all Christians are to be a minister. In the Bible the words "service" and "ministry" are the same word and "servant" and "minister" are the same word. So all of us are called to minister. So you say "I'm not called to ministry." Oh yes you are! If you are called to salvation, you are called to serve. God not

> only created us for service, He gave us a model in Jesus Christ. In Matthew 20:28 we read, "Jesus said, 'Your attitude must be like my own, for I did not come to be served, but to serve.'"

With regards to evangelism and mission, Warren says the following in his sermon entitled, "Made for a Mission."

> Evangelism is just the Greek word for "good news." The Bible says that once I know the Good News, that God loves me, has a purpose and plan for my life and all the things we've talked about, God wants me to pass it on, sharing the Good News with others. Where are we supposed to share it? Acts 1:8, says, "You will be my witnesses in Jerusalem, and in all Judea and Samaria, and to the ends of the earth." When Jesus told this to His followers, they were in Jerusalem. He was saying, first, I want you to start at home. I want you to start with the people closest to you, right there in your own city, your own community. Then he says I want you to go to Judea and Samaria, that's like the county next door, and Samaritans happen to be different culturally and different racially. God is building a family of people who love and trust Him, that are going to spend eternity with Him. That's the whole point of history. One day all believers are going to be gathered together in heaven. This is not Mission Impossible. It's Mission Inevitable. It's going to happen because it has been God's plan all along. Ephesians 3:11 says, "This was God's plan for all of history which He carried out through Christ Jesus, our Lord." The mission that Jesus Christ started when He came to earth, He says, "I want you guys to finish it." We're it. Being on this mission is the greatest privilege we're ever given, to be in on making history.

So to summarize what Rick Warren is saying, the mission of the Church is to complete the work of Jesus. Mission is the function of the local church and teens must learn they too have a responsibility to carry out the mission Christ gave us all. Ministry, service and evangelism are ways we carry out that mission. It requires serving other people using our God-given gifts and talents. As long as we are alive, we're to serve others and share the good news about Jesus. Evangelism is sharing the good news of what Jesus did for us when He died on the cross for our salvation. If we serve others, or minister to them, they are more open to hearing about the good news, that is, they are more open to our evangelism.

To do ministry: When asked why you should consider a mission tour, tell your group about the significance of being able to do ministry. It is a wonderful experience to be able to go into a community and share the gospel with a group of small children during a Vacation Bible School or a camp program, or as you work with a community on a construction project. As you serve in a soup kitchen or talk to street people, you will have opportunities to help those who need help and to share the good news of Jesus coming into the world.

When setting out to minister, we need to remember that service and evangelism together, are the best way to accomplish our mission. The biblical way of viewing both ministry and evangelism is as "two wings of the same bird." I first heard this from my former pastor at First Baptist Church, Dartmouth, Nova Scotia, James Chang. He said, "You cannot have one without the other." One does not lead to the other or become a means to display the other; rather, one cannot exist without the other. Ministry should be seen as a physical manifestation of evangelism. Feeding someone can become a physical way of presenting the gospel. People have material needs to which we should minister, and this ministry will convey the message of God's love.

A mission tour is a wonderful opportunity to take a group out of their normal environment so that they can take part in ministry and evangelism. A teen might be quite bold about sharing the gospel away from home, yet shyer about it within his or her community or school. By getting used to doing ministry and evangelism in a setting away from home, students may feel more confident about carrying out those same duties when they return. Going away provides a level of comfort as well as new and different ministry challenges.

You must be careful that you are not doing ministry that is a make work project to help you feel good about doing some work in the name of Jesus. When I took an exploratory trip to Houston, Texas, in March of 1998, prior to taking our entire team down in

July, the pastor of the host church questioned me at length about our group's sense of call. He commented that other groups come and visit and claim to be doing missions work during their time there, but he found that they were just putting in time to do their own thing under the guise of missions. He said that he never turned any group away, but if he felt that their number one goal was sightseeing and having fun, then he would find a task for them to do that would not have a negative impact on his church's witness in the area.

An example of this can be found in the article "Why Most Mission Trips Are a Waste of Time (And How to Make Sure Yours Isn't!)." The author, Noel Becchetti (1997), gives the following example: "A friend of mine has coordinated mission and service trips into northern Mexico for years. One of his sites is an orphanage, full of boys and girls dying for love and attention – and the Wall. 'I've got this Wall,' he told me. 'When a group comes that can't handle what's required to build relationships with Mexican kids, or insists on completing a task so they can 'accomplish' something, I put them to work on the Wall. They feel like they're a big help, and it keeps them out of everyone's hair so the ministry isn't compromised.'"

What Becchetti is saying is that the wall is a project with a different purpose for people he feels are problematic. These students feel as though they have made a contribution, even if their work is different from what the other students are doing.

Pray through what God wants your group to do in the way of ministry and evangelism before you set out to do ministry. It will make a lot of difference in the success of your mission tour effort. Here are some verses to reflect upon.

> *... and if you spend yourselves in behalf of the hungry and satisfy the needs of the oppressed, then your light will rise in the darkness, and your night will become like the noonday.*
>
> ISAIAH 58:10

> *... God was reconciling the world to himself in Christ, not counting men's sins against them. And he has committed to us the message of reconciliation.* 2 CORINTHIANS 5:19

To be ministered to: While being ministered to is not the goal of a mission tour, it is frequently the result. When you take your teens on a trip, you should incorporate times of worship and learning so this ministry can take place. If you are connected to a national mission tour or conference, teens will meet together for worship as indicated on the schedule. These contemporary worship events are designed especially for the teens, engaging them on their level in a way they might not have experienced in the past. The ministry of the worship team and the speaker will encourage growth in the students' spiritual life.

If you are doing a mission tour with only your group you will have to be intentional about these ministry times. A devotional and worship time should be shared each day. I've always made a point of having a Bible study time after lunch with our group where we study a lesson and use discussion questions to lead us into deeper concepts. Also, before everyone goes to bed for the evening, I like to engage the teens in deeper discussions about the events of the day, based on what we talked about in our study earlier. If possible, you can also incorporate a small worship time using a guitar or even a CD of worship music. This intimate study and worship time will help the team stay focused on the goal of the trip. They may need to be reminded that while they are benefiting from the overall experience, the trip is not for them. Their goal is to spread the good news about Jesus Christ and to do ministry.

> *Yet a time is coming and has now come when the true worshipers will worship the Father in spirit and truth, for they are the kind of worshipers the Father seeks. God is spirit and his worshipers must worship in spirit and in truth.* JOHN 4:23, 24

> *These commandments that I give you today are to be upon your hearts. Impress them on your children. Talk about them when you sit at home and when you walk along the road, when you lie down and when you get up.* DEUTERONOMY 6:6,7

To have fun: The fun refers to the fellowship times together. Sightseeing, amusement parks, restaurants and sporting activities can be built into the mission tour to provide an outlet for unwinding and relaxing. These times will provide opportunities for team members to minister to one another, to encourage and build one another up in a loving atmosphere. A lot of good memories can be made during these times, as each person reflects on the ministry that has taken place. Fellowship implies that you look after one another. If your church baptizes an individual into the body of Christ, you should do all you can to make them feel like a valued and accepted part of the body.

While "fun" is not the purpose of fellowship, fellowship can be fun. In most churches, we are guilty of describing church suppers and conversations as fellowship. The word fellowship is quite often misused, as are other words like worship, discipleship, ministry and evangelism. However, fun is often the doorway to relationships, which lead into deep and meaningful fellowship. Fun times, in any situation, build a sense of family and community and lead to memories that last for years to come. Fun activities within the fellowship of believers go a long way towards establishing relationships which can build one another up.

> Let us not give up meeting together, as some are in the habit of doing, but let us encourage one another – and all the more as you see the Day approaching. HEBREWS 10:25

You and your teens will get to know each other better in one week of mission than you will during an entire year of youth group activities: Teens will see you at your best and your worst as you work, sleep, eat and get along together. They will observe how you model the example of Jesus in your life, while you will learn more about them and how they live their lives. If you handle a particular situation very well, they will notice. If you make a huge mistake in one way or another, they will witness that as well. Afterwards, the way in which you deal with your mistakes is also important. We are all flawed individuals, imperfect and sinful in the sight of God and in need of turning to Him for forgiveness. When your teens are able to see you in weakness as well as strength, then you will have taught them how to cope in similar situations of their own.

In 1 Corinthians 4:8–21, Paul contrasts the troubles and distress of the apostles with the Corinthians and how highly they regarded themselves. He is showing them the example of humility displayed by the apostles and how they also need to be humble. You, as a youth leader, need to be willing to humble yourself in front of your teens. It will be difficult to put on your best face during every moment of a mission tour, so you need to be humble enough to share your flawed self with the group. They will get to know the real you during the short span of a mission tour and hopefully, the real you will reflect Jesus.

At the same time, you will get to know your teens. On mission tours, teens will tell you things about their life at home. You will discover the teens that suffer from situations of divorce, abuse, alcoholism, financial constraints or personal tragedies. You will also find out a lot of nice things about them, including their interests in sports, music, hobbies, part-time jobs and dating. They will tell you what they like and dislike about school and you can listen to them wrestle with their thoughts on future education and careers. They are more apt to discuss this on a long trip, as you travel together or work side by side for long hours each day. Being away from home also creates an openness and acceptance that fosters such conversations. Take advantage of these times with your teens. They are rare moments, but seem to occur more often when travelling together on a mission tour.

¶ Conclusion

To do ministry. To be ministered to. To have fun. These are the reasons for engaging teenagers in short-term mission. May God bless you as you prepare to lead your youth group in a life-changing short-term mission experience.

¶ References

Becchetti, N. (1997). Why Most Mission Trips Are a Waste of Time (And How to Make Sure Yours Isn't!). *Youthworker.* March/April 1997.

Fields, D. (1998). *Purpose Driven Youth Ministry.* Grand Rapids, MI: Zondervan.

4 Selecting and Building Support for a Mission Project

Bruce Fawcett & Rob Nylen

¶ Issues to consider when selecting a project

Perhaps the most important step involved in planning a mission project is the work that is done before the teenagers even hear about your plans. Carefully choosing a project that is appropriate for your group is a very important step that can go a long way toward guaranteeing a vibrant mission experience for your students.

Pray: If God cares enough to count the hairs on your head (Mathew 10:30) then surely you can be confident that God cares about the spiritual development of the teenagers you work with. If this is true you can pray with confidence, knowing that He will guide your plans each step of the way. It is very appropriate to pray at the beginning of the whole planning process a prayer as simple as this: *Lord, I know you care about these students even more than I do and I really believe that involvement in mission is key to their spiritual growth. So I ask you to guide my thoughts and plans through the whole process so that our project might honour you, allow us to mature spiritually and serve others effectively. Amen.*

Involving adult volunteer leaders: An integral part of a successful trip is having the right leaders. Although many may think recruitment for such a trip will be difficult, experience has shown that after one trip, volunteer leaders want to go every year. How do we ensure that this is also your experience?

a. *Pick leaders who compliment you:* You know your own strengths and weaknesses. If you are weak administratively, find a leader for whom this is their strength. If you struggle with budgets and expenses, bring along someone who likes to balance the books.

b. *Look for spiritual maturity and stability:* While, as group leader, you will be responsible for everyone on the trip, your leaders should not require a lot of maintenance. Look for individuals who demonstrate spiritual maturity and who are emotionally stable.

c. *Sell it well:* If you recruit by explaining a leader's role as a babysitter for five days, you will likely find recruitment difficult. If you make it sound like they will be on the front lines of ministry, able to watch the teens do new things for the first time in their life, and be able to experience God at work in a new way, then your recruitment will be easy. Visit a prospective leader's home, or take them out to lunch and try to communicate that you are approaching *them*, and only a privileged few would be asked.

d. *Tell the truth:* It is important that they know well in advance what is required of them as leaders. It is wise to write the expectations down and then present it to them with opportunity for discussion and negotiation. For example, one year a middle-aged couple told me they wanted to come, but needed good beds. I had to rent cots for them for the week and it was worth the money spent to have them on the trip. Others need to know what their responsibilities will be in regards to looking after youth, discipline and money spent. All of these clarifications may save you headaches later. One area you will want to think about is whether they are responsible for their own costs like accommodations, food and travel. Again, this should be clarified up front. It is our experience that leaders' costs should be covered by the church or by fundraising and your budget should reflect this. Most volunteers are taking their personal vacation time to travel and live with the teens and covering their costs is a fair trade.

e. *Treat them like leaders:* If they are going to own the trip and feel like an integral part of the experience, they should be in on decision making throughout. Their own wisdom and experience will enhance the trip for all. They will likely be interested in holding responsibility for part of the week's events. One year a leader wanted to lead all the morning devotions, another was an accountant and handled the finances, another was a nurse and handled all medicines and planned a healthy menu. If they have signed up to help, use them.

f. *Debrief with them regularly:* On the trip it is wise to have daily meetings at the start and end of each day. Look over the plan for the day and ensure everyone is on the same page. At the end of the day have a time of celebration and reflection on how things went. At the end of the trip, it is also wise to get their feedback and to tell the stories of the event.

g. *Consider them possible recruits:* As a rule, most youth pastors will invite their weekly youth leaders to have first dibs on coming on the mission tour. Often they want to come, some may want a break. If you are taking new volunteer leaders, and they are willing to give up their vacation time to travel and live with teens then they may be potential youth group leaders down the line. Watch them closely to see if they respond to the teens and how the teens respond to them. When you debrief them at the end of the trip, see if they are open to involvement throughout the year. Remember, from the teens' perspective, these leaders have been present with them during a highpoint in their life and may strongly welcome them into the weekly youth ministry activities.

Selecting students for the team: The next step in choosing a project that is appropriate for your group is to gain a realistic understanding of who will make up your team. It is wise to take a piece of paper and write down the students that you think will take part in a proposed mission tour. The tendency for a youth leader is to be overly optimistic in guessing how many of your students are ready and available for such an initiative. When making your guess, take into account the need for some students to work in the summer and that those on the fringes of your group may be shy about agreeing to go on a trip.

Assess your potential team: After making your list, take a good look at your potential team members and ask yourself some important questions: Are they mostly junior high or high school students? Do they have mission experience or not? Are they mostly upfront leaders – people who are comfortable being in charge – or alongside leaders who are more comfortable being helpers? Are they strong in their Christian faith for their age or new converts? What are their gifts and talents? If your potential team is mostly young with little experience and tend not to be upfront leaders, you probably should be thinking more about a work camp experience rather than street witnessing! At the same time, if your team will likely be made up of veteran high school students who have mission experience, then maybe you ought to consider a cross-cultural experience in Atlantic Canada, a major Canadian urban centre or overseas.

Youth only vs. intergenerational: Typically, most mission teams in Atlantic Canada primarily involve youth with a few leaders who plan and lead the trip. Another model which some churches are adopting is to invite more adults or even families to be a part of their mission team, creating a more intergenerational approach to mission. There are benefits to both models and your church simply needs to weigh out both your church's preference and the preference of the teenagers in your group. For churches that have had a primarily youth-focused mission emphasis in the past, you will need to be careful that your students do not feel that their program has been hijacked if you decide to move to a more intergenerational approach. Some churches may wish to send out two mission teams: a youth team and a team made up of families.

Large group, solo, partnership: The next major question you should ask when planning your mission project is: Should my group go on its mission project alone, should we partner with another group, or should we be part of a big group activity? There are merits to all of these possible arrangements and it would be wonderful for teenagers to experience all of these models of mission during their youth group experience.

a. *Large group:* As noted elsewhere is this book, there is incredible value in being part of a large-scale mission project like Tidal Impact. These projects are very adaptable and no matter where your group is at in terms of gifting, age, and experience, a project with an appropriate level of challenge can be designed for them. Since these large projects are not annual events it is wise to take advantage of them when they are offered. These projects are helpful for all groups, but they are especially valuable to beginning leaders. Enough of a structure exists that you are virtually guaranteed a positive experience and you will not be responsible for planning all activities or ministries for your own group for the whole week. On the so-called "off years", when a major project is not being held, there are two other ways that you can offer a mission experience to your teenagers.

b. *Solo project:* Your group could decide to go it alone and engage in a mission project by itself. The greatest strength of this choice is that you can totally design your experience with your group in mind and you can use the experience as a bonding time for your own group. There are all sorts of things you could do. Perhaps if your group is younger and less experienced, you could visit a summer camp and help the staff prepare for the opening of the camp by painting, cutting the grass and doing odd jobs. If your group is a little more experienced you could visit a smaller church in a more isolated area and assist them with a children's outreach project. If your group is very experienced they could be involved in a cross-cultural project in a major city. All of these types of experiences and many more are possible as long as you start your planning early.

c. *Partnership:* If you did not want to go it alone, you could also partner with another group. If you are a volunteer leader and a first-time mission tour leader it might be wise to ask a local youth pastor if your group could pair up with his or her group and go on a mission project together. This would give you the peace of mind of working with a more experienced leader and would allow you to learn the ropes so you could lead a team of your own the next year. You could also partner with another group as a visiting or host church. In this model of partnership it is also possible for an experienced group to pair up with a less-experienced group in order to help the less-experienced group gain confidence.

If you are not able to think of anything yourself here are some ideas:

- Contact the Convention's Youth and Family Ministries department for ideas.
- Contact the denominational offices in a city you might like to visit. They can be found on the internet and will have helpful suggestions for you.
- Contact Canadian Baptist Ministries *www.cbmin.org*. They offer short-term mission trips and may have one that fits your group.
- Contact your colleagues to see where they have gone and what they learned for their own experience.

What ever you decide, you will want to ensure that there is a legitimate need and that your group is the right match to assist that need.

¶ Getting Others on Board

Even the best laid plans run amuck when they are not presented well. It is very important to explain to the appropriate stakeholders what you are planning and why. The newer you are to leadership and the newer the concept of a mission tour to your church, the more you will need to concentrate on explaining your vision and plans.

The pastor: You should begin with the pastor. It is wise, at the start of the whole planning process, to make an appointment with the pastor and tell him or her that you are thinking about leading a mission tour for some of the teenagers in your group. You should explain that you'd like to explore options and return in a couple of months with a proposal. Once you have your proposal ready you should return to the pastor with your plan and invite suggestions for improving the ideas. Pastors often have the necessary ministry experience and congregational understanding that can sharpen your plan and help you avoid rookie mistakes.

The board: Your next step should be to request time at the next board meeting to present your plan. Perhaps you should meet with the Board of Deacons or the Board of Christian Education or both. Your pastor can suggest what would be appropriate. A PowerPoint presentation should allow you to communicate a fair amount of information in a short period of time so that all can understand and digest your material well. It is worth your time to prepare a thorough presentation so that you can be sure that people understand your vision. Your goals in meeting with the board should be to:

- Help them understand the rationale for youth mission projects
- Help them understand your particular proposal
- Answer obvious questions such as cost, timing, safety factors and leadership

If you feel there might be a little resistance from the board for some reason it might be wise to bring in an outside "expert" to talk about the value of involving youth in mission. Perhaps your guest could be a neighbouring youth pastor who has led many trips, or a denominational staff person or youth ministry professor. A visitor may help your church leadership understand not only the importance of mission tours but also the fact that they are an integral part of leading youth programs all across North America. He or she can also suggest that by adding a mission tour to your program you hope your teenagers will have the same growth opportunities as students in other churches.

Parents: Once you gain the endorsement of the board you should arrange a meeting with the parents of teenagers in your group. It is very important to gain the support of the parents before inviting teenagers to be part of your mission project. Sometimes in youth ministry parents feel out of the loop. On a major issue such as a long trip away it is essential that parents hear about the plans before their daughters and sons. While they should not have veto rights over the whole proposal, individual parents may have valuable insight into your plan that can make your proposal sharper. Parents need to feel that they were consulted and that you did not do an end-run around them.

It is very important for you to consider carefully what parents you would like to meet with. If your students come primarily from homes where the parents don't go to church, you may not want to have a general parents meeting to ask for their blessing on your mission tour. These parents may not understand or agree with your rationale and thus may attempt to torpedo your vision. Rather than a general mailing to parents in which you invite them to a parents meeting, it is usually wise to announce a parents meeting from the pulpit on a Sunday morning and arrange to meet with church-going parents following a Sunday service.

Parents are sometimes no better at keeping a secret than students, so if you do not want parents telling their children what you talked to them about, you had better explain to them what to say when their son or daughter asks what the meeting was about. If you want to build a little momentum then you can simply instruct parents to say, "Your youth leader has a very exciting plan to share with you at your next meeting. When you hear it I think you are going to be really excited." The longer the span of time between the parents meeting and the next meeting with your teenagers, the greater the opportunity that the teenagers will find out before you tell them.

Students: Assuming that you have gained the approval and blessing of the pastor, the church board and the parents of your teenagers, it is now time to invite your students to take part in your mission tour. If your students are used to going on a mission tour every summer, then the goal of your presentation is simply to explain to them the nature of this year's project and why it is important for them to be involved.

If your students have never been involved in mission before and the whole concept is new to your church, then you need to think carefully about how to explain your vision. Don't assume that because it seems like a great idea to you that it necessarily will be to them!

Your first step is to help them understand the rationale for being involved in mission in the first place. It may be a good idea to do all or some of the following:

a. Invite a high school student who has been involved in youth mission tours for some time to come and share with your group about their experiences and how God used mission in their life.

b. Show a video to help students understand what you mean by a mission tour. If you are planning to be involved in Tidal Impact, contact the Convention of Atlantic Baptist Churches to get the most recent retrospective video.

c. Plan a series of Bible studies for your teens on mission and service in the weeks leading up to launching your mission tour publicly.

d. Ask someone of stature from your congregation whom your students respect to come in and make a joint presentation with you.

e. Take them on a weekend mission tour to introduce them to what mission is all about before you invite them to take on an even greater commitment.

f. Raise the possibility of a mission tour with a couple of key opinion leaders in your group and get their reaction to the idea before telling the whole group.

Once you feel that there is a solid base on which to make a presentation and there is general consensus that involvement in mission is a good thing, it is time to explain the project. Simply tell the teenagers with energy and enthusiasm why you feel that this would be a great experience for them. Explain your plans for the project in detail. Tell them that you will help them get ready so they feel prepared and that you will help them come up with the money if that is an issue for them.

Congregation: Since you will likely be going to the congregation to ask for prayer and financial support for your mission tour, it is very important to bring them into the loop as well. Perhaps you could ask for time at the annual meeting to talk about your plans or maybe you could have some time during a Sunday service to make a presentation to the congregation. The pastor can decide with you what is best. It is also a good idea to give the program visibility in front of the congregation throughout the planning process, right up to a commissioning service the Sunday before your mission team leaves.

¶ Conclusion

Leading a mission tour involves more that just taking teenagers away for a week. It involves the careful selection of a project and thorough explanation of it to all stakeholders. If you plan and explain your vision well, you can have a mission tour where everyone feels that they have been consulted and have had their say, resulting in broad congregational support for your initiative. To skip steps and "do it the easy way" could result in a poorly planned project in which the congregation feels no ownership, thus depriving your teenagers of the visibility and support they need to help make the mission tour a success and spiritual milestone in their lives.

5 Making the Most of Tidal Impact

Rob Nylen

Tidal Impact is a youth mission event unique to Atlantic Canada. Built around a longing to realize missional youth ministries, Atlantic hospitality and a passion to strengthen the local church, Tidal Impact has formed the backbone of youth work in our region. Chapter 17 gives an historic outline of Tidal Impact, its roots and its context, so in this chapter we want to answer the question, "How can my group make the most of Tidal Impact?"

¶ Understanding the Timeline

The planning committee starts planning Tidal Impact two years in advance, and it is recommended that the local church start planning one year in advance. A local church youth leadership team will want to make the formal decision to be involved in Tidal Impact in late summer or early fall (one year prior), and start to anticipate how it will affect your fall youth ministry. Here are some things to consider:

Tidal Impact will give focus to your ministry: As a youth leader, you can build your weekly discipleship ministry around preparing for Tidal Impact. We have included a chapter on *The Discipleship Project* which gives you an example you can modify and implement. Teens are always more keen to prepare when they know what they are preparing for.

Budget implications: Knowing by September where your summer mission tour will be can allow you adequate time to raise necessary funds and allow parents adequate time to set funds aside for the teens registration fee. The program fee for a one-week mission tour like Tidal Impact is normally under $125 per person. This fee, paid by both students and leaders, covers admission to all evening rallies and fun events, a couple of group meals, a t-shirt, a commemorative DVD mailed post-event, admission to all afternoon events and all administrative costs. Groups who attend look after their own transportation costs and normally have to pay for a few suppers during the event itself.

Allows time to enlist congregational support: Preparing for Tidal Impact can and should involve your entire congregation. You should view Tidal Impact as an opportunity to build bridges with the rest of the church family. Here are some suggestions: gather prayer partners for your youth, involve your church in necessary fundraising, ask your church to commission your teens and most importantly, ask if you can have a Sunday worship service following Tidal Impact so you can share how God was at work during their week of mission.

Tidal Impact is full by Christmas: Tidal Impact fills quickly and is typically full by the Christmas before the event. Registering late will have complicating implications: your team may have to be broken in two and minister in two separate locations, you may not be able to go to the location of your choice, all your team may not be able to come, or you may be turned away entirely.

Establishing partnerships: Tidal Impact is built around two churches partnering together. Once you have registered, we will help you find a ministry partner based on your church's size and experience. Many groups already have an idea of a church they would like to partner with.

❡ Understanding the Purpose

There are several purposes to this event:

Tidal Impact is a time of service: In a culture that promotes selfish lifestyles, we want our teens to discover that life is found when we give it away. Each year our teens touch thousands of lives and leave a God-imprint in their area.

Tidal Impact is an Acts 2 discipleship experience: If you remember the early church community, as described in Acts 2, you can visualize them eating together, sharing communion, taking time to study God's word, serving others, meeting the needs of each other, and joining for worship. This also describes a week at Tidal Impact, an Acts 2 experience. We immerse your teens in a week of mission, discipleship and celebration and watch God work.

Tidal Impact creates community: Partnerships between churches allow your teens to meet Christian youth from across the region and the country. Many keep in touch and form friendships that last into the college years.

Tidal Impact creates a positive experience with local churches: Often, in youth culture, the value of the local church is not seen. A week of service, rubbing shoulders with local church volunteers, and experiencing first hand the hospitality from a local congregation can create a positive perspective.

❡ Understanding Partnerships

Tidal Impact is successful when partnerships are successful. The event is built on partnerships between host and visiting churches. If a church is located where the event is held, they are a host church. Groups travelling more then one hour from the host location are visiting churches. In most cases, after a host church has registered, they will call a ministry colleague and invite them to come and join them in a week of service. This happens for all the host churches in the area, creating a teaming up that is like no other mission event in Canada. These local church partnerships create a synergy and excitement that lasts beyond the event. A partnership includes three components for the host church:

Billets: Your church will have the privilege of hosting the visiting team. You need to start by deciding how many your church can billet. Visiting students should always be billeted in groups of two or more, and they should always be of the same gender. Billeting requires the 3 B's: a bed each, breakfast and a bag lunch each day. The youth may also need to be dropped off at the morning ministry site. To make billeting easier, you may request that the visiting youth fill out cue cards with their name, lunch preferences and any allergies listed. This will help your hosts be best prepared.

Evening meals: Tidal Impact will offer two evening meals that all are invited to attend. You, as the host, will be required to feed your visitors on the other evenings. You should plan these evening meals in consultation with the visiting team. Often there are other groups within the church who would enjoy preparing these meals. Mission groups, Sunday School teachers or parents often enjoy serving in this way. It may be necessary for the visiting church to bring some financial assistance to help cover the costs of these meals. Again, this should be worked out in advance and will vary given the amount of teens coming and the types of meals prepared.

Communication: It is typically the responsibility of the host church to make sure they have communicated all information to their visiting team. Constant communication will make this event a success. You should invite their leaders to come and visit your church in advance, to meet your leaders and get a sense of the community. You should start talking about ministry, meals, transportation, billeting and free time right away. Constant communication will ensure nothing is forgotten and nothing is assumed.

¶ Understanding the Schedule

If you look at Appendix 7 at the back of this book, you will see an example of a schedule from Tidal Impact in 2004. Note the shaded areas are timeslots that the Tidal Impact committee has prepared something for your team to participate in. The unshaded areas are the time slots where you are responsible to decide what your group will be doing. Lets look at the unshaded areas you are responsible for:

Morning ministry: Tidal Impact provides a framework whereby local churches can make the most of serving their community. The schedule for the week encourages local churches to connect as often as possible with their community through acts of service. An example is morning ministries. Each local church must decide what ministry they are going to undertake during the mornings. Many save their Vacation Bible School for the week of Tidal Impact, knowing the extra youth helpers will be greatly appreciated. Other churches use the extra help to assist them in doing a new type of outreach: sports camp, computer camp, or Backyard Bible Clubs. The morning ministry is the complete responsibility of the local church.

Once you have chosen your morning ministry, you must decide which responsibilities your church will carry, and which ones you would like your visitors to undertake. It is best if you have the resources in enough time to send to your visiting team so they can have adequate time to prepare. Some elements of a morning ministry are best carried out by the local church: snacks and registration while others are easily handled by the visiting team: crafts, games or Bible stories. If your church is unable to staff a morning ministry at all, then you might ask your visitors to come and use the Vacation Bible School they used at their own church previously that summer. Regardless, make sure you communicate clearly with your visitors so they can provide what you need.

Sunday morning: You will have your guests on a Sunday morning, and you should think of how they can be involved in the morning service. These morning services often provide an exciting start to the week and will be remembered as a highlight of the summer.

Afternoon ministries: The Tidal Impact local planning committee will divide all the local teams and their hosts into *groups A, B, or C.* This will mean each group will consist of 150–225 people. After you have registered, the local organizing committee will send you a letter (and post it on the *tidalimpact.ca* site) to let you know what group you are in. If you look at Appendix 7, we will assume your mission team is in group A. Each afternoon, we provide a framework for you to be involved in a *ministry elective and park ministry*.

a. *Ministry Electives:* We want to encourage your group to connect with a local agency where you can volunteer for the afternoon. Some groups make arrangements at a nursing home, a community centre, do a food drive, volunteer at a food bank or soup kitchen. As you make these plans, you should consider the size of your group and the type of skills required. If you cannot find a place for your team to serve, the local planning committee will assist you. These plans are made in February or March prior to the event.

b. *Park Ministry:* As with *ministry electives,* we want to encourage your teens to go public with their gifts. The Tidal Impact committee will locate appropriate public venues, and will look after a sound system and an emcee, but you are required to prepare your team with an appropriate presentation and to communicate what your group will be doing. We would ask you to consider these presentations as *planting events,* simply, an opportunity to share the good news of Jesus Christ. These presentations should not be too aggressive in tone nor should the presenters be too "churchy" in the language they use.

Evening Fun Event: One of the evenings during the week will be a night off. This much required down time should be enjoyed. Your teens will be tired and in need of some recreation. Do not over plan the night. The best fun events are ones where teens can swim, visit and just hang out.

Now let's look at the shaded boxes, the events during the week that we prepare for you, so you can make the most of these experiences:

1. *Evening Rallies:* It has been our experience that the evening rallies provide an amazing opportunity for the youth to passionately respond to what God has been doing. The youth serve all day and come to the evening rallies to offer thanks and to be encouraged to head out in the morning for another day of ministry. These evenings offer high energy worship, strong Biblical teaching, opportunities for youth to use their gifts and a chance to hear stories of what God is doing elsewhere in the event.

    a. *Combined Rallies:* Although Tidal Impact is in two locations simultaneously, it has been our practice to join together twice during the week so the youth can get a sense of the size of the event. The tradition has been to open these combined rallies to the public so they can join the celebration and see what the event is about.

    b. *Evening Communion Service:* Each year, at an evening rally near the end of the week, we share in a special service of communion. This night provides an amazing opportunity for youth to wrestle with God's call on their lives to live missionally year-round.

Afternoon concerts of prayer: Your group will have an opportunity to gather together with others during an afternoon concert of prayer. These prayer events are led by the Atlantic Baptist Youth Executive, a young adult leadership team. Here youth can pray for their families, the ministries they are involved in during the week, and the other youth who are out serving in the community. There is a worship team who helps facilitate this prayer time as well.

Afternoon fun events: We recognize the need for students to unwind during the week. We provide a fun event open to all registrants. Previous fun events have been a water theme park, an exhibition, laser-tag and mini putt or organized beach activities.

Group suppers: Twice during the week, Tidal Impact provides a supper for all registrants. These provide an opportunity to build community among the teens and also take some of the meal related work off of the local church. These suppers are typically provided by a sponsoring group such as Atlantic Baptist University or Acadia Divinity College.

As you can see, Tidal Impact has a variety of Acts 2 elements during the week. We hope that knowing about them early on, will help you make the most of this event as you seek to cultivate the Christ-life in your youth.

Tidal Impact is every two years in a different location. We believe it provides leaders an opportunity to bring their youth to an event which is a guaranteed success. We also believe it offers a healthy balance of "already planned" elements as well as an opportunity to tailor this week to your group. There were 109 different groups involved in Tidal Impact 2004 and each group had a unique and dynamic experience. Each group had different morning ministries in different types of communities. Each group was in different parks and went different places for their evening off. Although Tidal Impact is a "big group event" there is plenty of opportunity to use the event to accomplish great things.

❡ Concluding Story

One of my greatest memories from Tidal Impact 2000, held in Halifax, was seeing God change Jason's life. Jason had not fully dedicated his life to the Lord, but it was during a time of commitment at one of the evening rallies that Jason walked forward signifying his intent to dedicate his life to Christ. This had been stirring in Jason's heart for some time, but the Lord used the circumstances and people from Tidal Impact to do His work. The story continues.

Jason's mom was a leader for the event, and was the first person at Jason's side when he went forward. It was a powerful moment for he and his mom and our group. At Tidal Impact 2004, Jason was a group leader for his local church. Thursday night during communion Jason approached me with a young girl from his youth group who asked for prayer. She was wrestling with some issues that she had been convicted of during the event and had turned to Jason, who was now a leader. It was so amazing to see Jason, once a youth, now a leader, taking youth, leading them in prayer and acting as a spiritual role model in the group. It reminds me these events create opportunities for God to challenge and change the lives of those involved, including the youth, the leaders, and the organizers. God has done amazing things through this event, and we have no reason to believe He is finished.

6 Mission Tour Participants: Who are they?

Bruce Fawcett

¶ Introduction

Most youth leaders who have led short-term mission trips have noticed that not all youth are attracted to, or interested in, such an experience. Sometimes we are glad that not everyone wants to be part of our team, other times we had hoped for more interest than we received. Research reveals that the idea of a short-term mission experience appeals to a certain type of youth. The goal of this chapter is to provide a snapshot of the kind of youth who are attracted to short-term mission by painting a portrait of the youth who attended Tidal Impact 2002 in Moncton and Saint John, New Brunswick.

This portrait is obtained from a survey completed by 792 youth during Tidal Impact 2002. This data will be reported in the following categories: the sample, home and school, religious background, public religious practices, and private religious practices. In this analysis percentages have been rounded to the nearest whole number. Percentages of .4% or below were rounded down and percentages of .5% or above were rounded up and thus percentages do not always add up to 100%.

¶ The Sample

Gender

TABLE 6.01 What is your gender?	
GENDER	TOTAL (%)
Male	35%
Female	65%

The Tidal Impact youth were asked to indicate whether they are male or female.

Given the results from other surveys of Baptist youth in Atlantic Canada, it was not surprising that there were more females (65%) than males (35%) in attendance at Tidal Impact 2002. For instance, in a survey of youth groups affiliated with the Convention of Atlantic Baptist Churches ("the Convention") in 1999, I discovered (Fawcett 2000) that females outnumbered males by nearly two to one. Likewise, in a survey conducted at the Springforth youth conference in May 2002, 59% of the attendees in Grades 9–12 reported that they were female (Fawcett and Linkletter, 2003). Both Tidal Impact and Springforth are sponsored by the Convention.

The smaller number of males in youth groups and at large youth events should remind youth leaders of the importance of having male youth group leaders so that the youth see that Christian faith is relevant to adult males as well as adult females. Youth group leaders may also wish to consider the possibility of holding occasional male-only events to put a greater focus on building the male percentage of attendees in their youth group.

Age

The youth were asked to indicate their age at the time of Tidal Impact.The vast majority of the males (66%) and females (75%) were 13, 14, 15 or 16 years old. The smaller number of attendees 12 years old and under may be due to the fact that Grade 6 students in New Brunswick are generally included in church youth groups, whereas Grade 6 students in some other Atlantic Provinces are not. This results from the fact that New Brunswick schools organize their older grades by middle school (Grades 6–8) and high school (Grades 9–12) groupings rather than by junior high school (Grades 7–9) and high school (Grades 10–12) groupings like most other Atlantic Provinces. It is also possible that parents or youth leaders of some 12 year olds thought that they may be too young to attend a weeklong event and thus 12 year olds may not have been included in some of the church mission teams.

TABLE 6.02 How old are you?

AGE	MALE (%)	FEMALE (%)
12 & under	10%	9%
13	17%	18%
14	16%	25%
15	13%	19%
16	20%	13%
17	15%	11%
18	9%	6%

The percentage of attendees for each age band drops after age 16 for males and age 15 for females. A likely explanation for there being fewer youths with each succeeding year of age is that once a student is 16, he or she usually seeks summer employment. With the steady rise in the cost of post-secondary education it is likely that some youth, as they get older and closer to university entrance, face more encouragement from their parents to seek employment in the summer rather than attend a weeklong summer event like Tidal Impact. It has also been demonstrated that in Atlantic Canada, church youth group attendance drops off significantly in high school (Fawcett, 2000). This drop off in attendance should encourage churches to consider carefully whether the level of challenge in their programming and teaching is high enough for those in high school. In addition, churches may also wish to consider dividing their group into separate junior high and high school groups as soon as they have the critical mass to do so. This would allow the two separate programs to take on a feel of their own and ensure that the youth are not being invited to attend the same program for seven years.

Place of Residence

TABLE 6.03 Where do you live?

PLACE OF RESIDENCE	MALE (%)	FEMALE (%)
Newfoundland	3	1
Prince Edward Island	6	2
New Brunswick	57	60
Nova Scotia	26	27
Quebec	0	1
Ontario	7	5
Alberta	0	2
Other Canadian Province/Territory	0	0
United States	1	2
Europe	0	0

The youth were asked where they lived. While Tidal Impact participants came from a variety of provinces, the vast majority originated from New Brunswick (57% male, 60% female) and Nova Scotia (26% male, 27% female). The fact that most of the youth originated from New Brunswick was not a surprise. The hosting area for Tidal Impact 2002 was southern New Brunswick and thus every visiting youth mission team needed to be hosted by a church from New Brunswick. In addition, according to the *2002 Directory of the Convention of Atlantic Baptist Churches*, 242 of the 550 churches that are affiliated with the Convention are located in New Brunswick. The fact that Nova Scotia was the home province to many of the youth could be due to the fact that the previous Tidal Impact, held in 2000, had been in Nova Scotia and thus many of the youth from that locale were familiar with the event. In addition, 280 churches of the 550 churches affiliated with the Convention are located in Nova Scotia, providing a large base of local churches from which to recruit youth mission teams to attend Tidal Impact.

❡ Home and School

Parents divorced or separated?

Those surveyed were asked whether their parents had been divorced or separated. While 20% of the males and females reported that their parents had been divorced or separated, 80% said they had not. Males and females were equally as likely to have divorced parents. Statistics Canada (*www.statscan.ca*) reports that 37.7% of marriages in Canada end in divorce with the vast majority of these divorces involving dependant children. This suggests that the youth attending Tidal Impact are more likely than the youth of the general population to come from homes that have not experienced divorce. Even though the rate of divorce is lower than in the general population the percentage of divorce is still high enough to remind youth leaders that their youth need to see healthy marriages informally and be taught formally about the nature of Christian marriage.

TABLE 6.04 Have your parents been divorced or separated?

PARENTS DIVORCED/ SEPARATED	MALE (%)	FEMALE (%)
Yes	20	20
No	80	80

Average grade

The respondents were asked to report their academic performance in school. An astounding 53% of males and 73% of females indicated that their average grade was in the "A" category, with the next largest group (29% male, 21% of female) reporting an average grade of "B." Very few of the

TABLE 6.05 On your report card, what is your average grade?

GRADE	MALE (%)	FEMALE (%)
A 80% or higher or "A"	53	73
B 70% – 79% or "B"	29	21
C 60% – 69% or "C"	12	5
D 50% – 59% or "D"	5	1
F 49% or lower or "F"	0	0

youth reported average grades of "C" or "D." It is not clear whether church youth groups generally attract high academic achievers or whether this event attracts high achievers from within the various youth groups. However, it is clear that the invitation to be involved in a mission event such as Tidal Impact has a strong appeal for academically-able Christian youth, especially those who are female. The event's appeal to the academically-able youth is not surprising since many of the groups require a rigorous preparation program as part of their team's preparations for Tidal Impact.

It is not likely that summer school programs, which provide an opportunity for students to attempt to pass courses that they did not pass in the normal school year, had an effect on the attendance of less academically-able students. This is due to the fact that most summer school programs would have taken place during July and not the month of August when Tidal Impact 2002 was held.

School Program

Respondents were also asked what school program they were enrolled in. The data indicates that 29% of males and 40% of females were enrolled in either early or late French immersion, whereas 62% of males and 51% of females reported that they were enrolled in an English program. The remaining students were either enrolled in a French program or another type of program.

TABLE 6.06
What school program are you in?

PROGRAM	MALE (%)	FEMALE (%)
English	62	51
Early French Immersion	10	16
Late French Immersion	19	24
French	3	6
Other	4	3

Most early French immersion programs in Atlantic Canada start in Grade 1, whereas late French immersion programs generally start in Grade 6 or 7, depending on the province of residence. Both programs are intended to assist native English speakers develop a high level of French language proficiency. According to the official web site of the French immersion advocacy group, Canadian Parents for French (*http://www.cpfnb.com*), 27% of the students in the New Brunswick public school system in 2002 were enrolled in French immersion, the highest percentage of any province in Canada. Thus Tidal Impact attracted a disproportionately high percentage of students from French immersion programs, which are generally recognized as more demanding academic programs than the English-based programs. Again, the data highlights the attraction of this event for high academic achievers, especially females.

The high grades and prevalence of French immersion programs among these youth should again remind youth leaders to carefully consider the level of challenge they offer both in teaching and in programming. These youth are highly able and many can handle more challenging programming and teaching than is offered in many youth groups. The drop out rate noted in Table 6.02 may suggest, among other things, that those who are not challenged simply fade away.

¶ Religious Background

Parents as worshippers

The youth were asked whether or not their fathers and mothers attend Sunday worship regularly.

The vast majority of the youth (65% male, 60% female) reported that their father attended Sunday worship nearly every week. Only 12% of males and 17% of females reported that their father never attended worship. For some unclear reason, males were more likely (65%) than females (60%) to have fathers who attended Sunday wor-

TABLE 6.07 Does your father attend Sunday worship regularly?

FATHER ATTEND WORSHIP	MALE (%)	FEMALE (%)
Nearly every week	65	60
At least once a month	6	7
Sometimes	8	8
Once or twice a year	9	9
Never	12	17

ship nearly every week and conversely, females (17%) were much more likely than males (12%) to have fathers who never attended Sunday worship.

As noted in Table 6.08, the vast majority of the males (80%) and females (73%) indicated that their mothers attended Sunday worship nearly every week. Only 5% of males and 9% of females said their mothers never attend Sunday worship. Mothers are much more likely than fathers to be regular worship attendees with 83% of males and 77% of females reporting an attendance frequency of at least once a month or greater for the mothers, whereas only 71% of males and 67% of females reported a similar frequency rate for their fathers.

TABLE 6.08 Does your mother attend Sunday worship regularly?

MOTHER ATTEND WORSHIP	MALE (%)	FEMALE (%)
Nearly every week	80	73
At least once a month	3	4
Sometimes	9	6
Once or twice a year	4	7
Never	5	9

That data concerning parental involvement in worship reminds youth leaders of three key truths. First, many secular parents are still very open to their children being involved in Christian youth programs. Second, youth can, and often do, exhibit a higher level of spiritual practice than their parents. Third, faithful parents appear to breed faithful children. Parents who attend worship regularly are far more likely than the population at large to have teenagers who attend worship regularly.

¶ Public Religious Practices

Denomination

The respondents were asked to indicate to what denomination their youth group belonged. The vast majority of youth at Tidal Impact (94% male, 95% female) indicated that their youth group belonged to a Baptist denomination. The large percentage of Baptists may be explained by several factors.

First, Statistics Canada (*www.statscan.ca*) reports that, according to the 2001 Census, Baptists are the largest Protestant denomination in New Brunswick and Nova Scotia, the provinces of origin of 86% of attendees.

TABLE 6.09 What denomination does your youth group belong to?

DENOMINATION	MALE (%)	FEMALE (%)
Anglican	2	0
Associated Gospel Churches (AGC)	1	0
Baptist	94	95
Wesleyan	0	1
Other	4	4

Second, and perhaps most importantly, the event was sponsored by the Convention of Atlantic Baptist Churches and thus Baptists may have felt a stronger relationship with the event. Perhaps churches of other denominations felt hesitant about attending an event sponsored by Baptists.

Third, events of this type had been cultivated as part of the Baptist youth ministry culture over the previous decade. This allows Baptist youth groups to anticipate and prepare for such an event, whereas many youth groups in other denominations may not have been aware of Tidal Impact or anticipating it with the same level of excitement.

Church Location

TABLE 6.10 Where is your youth group's church building located?

CHURCH LOCATION	MALE (%)	FEMALE (%)
City	43	43
Suburb	11	8
Town	24	24
Village	14	16
Rural	8	8

The youth were asked to indicate where their church building is located. The sample was nearly equally divided between city and suburban youth (54% male, 51% female) versus youth from small towns, villages, and rural areas (46% male, 48% female). These figures ought to remind churches that youth ministry is not merely an urban or a suburban reality. Successful youth ministry is carried out in rural areas and villages as well as in city centers.

Youth Pastor

TABLE 6.11 Does your youth group have a paid youth pastor?

PAID YOUTH PASTOR	MALE (%)	FEMALE (%)
Yes	81	81
No	20	19

The respondents were asked to indicate whether their church employs a youth pastor to oversee their church's ministry to youth. The vast majority of the youth at Tidal Impact 2002 (81% of the males and females) indicated that a paid professional leads the youth ministry at their church. This number is incredibly high since while over 204 churches affiliated with the Convention of Atlantic Baptist Churches report having a youth group (Gardner, 2002), only 66 of these churches had paid staff in 2002 to oversee their youth ministry (Fawcett and Linkletter, 2003). Thus only 32% of Convention churches with youth groups employ a youth pastor and only 12% of the 550 Convention churches employ a youth pastor. The Tidal Impact program then attracts a disproportionate number of youth groups that are overseen by youth pastors. This may be explained simply by the fact that helping a group prepare for a weeklong mission tour and leading a group of youth on such a trip requires a significant amount of time and dedication. Many churches may not have a volunteer youth leader or pastor who is prepared or able to lead such an undertaking.

Sunday Worship Attendance

The youth were asked whether they attend Sunday worship in their church.The vast majority of the youth (90% male, 88% female) indicated that they attend Sunday worship in their church nearly every week. This figure is even higher than the 81% of the students participating in the Grade 9–12 Springforth youth conference in 2002 who reported that they attend Sunday worship nearly every week (Fawcett and Linkletter, 2003).

This figure is also vastly higher than the church attendance pattern of adolescents in the general Canadian population. According to the Statistics Canada publication *Youth in Canada* (3rd edition), in 1999 only 17% of 15–19 year olds in Canada attend religious services at least once a week. The high level of commitment to Sunday worship on the part of the Tidal Impact youth may be explained in part by the nature of the event itself. The invitation to teach the Christian faith to children, participate in social action programs, and engage in large group worship (Fawcett and McDonald, 2001) likely has a greater appeal to frequent church goers than to those who are infrequent church attendees. The high level of Sunday worship attendance also may be explained by the fact that some groups would have required regular Sunday attendance for those teens that wanted to be a part of their Tidal Impact team.

TABLE 6.12 Do you attend Sunday worship?

SUNDAY WORSHIP ATTENDANCE	MALE (%)	FEMALE (%
Nearly every week	90	88
At least once a month	3	4
Sometimes	7	7
Once or twice a year	0	1
Never	1	1

Same Church / Youth Group

The youth were asked to indicate whether they attended Sunday worship in the same church where they attended youth group. Most of the youth (91% male and 88% female) indicated that they attended a youth group in the same church as the one they worshipped in on Sunday. As noted earlier, 99% of the youth reported (Table 6.12) that they attended Sunday worship somewhere. It is likely that those who

TABLE 6.13 Do you attend Sunday worship in the same church you attend youth group?

SAME CHURCH/ YOUTH GROUP	MALE (%)	FEMALE (%)
Yes	91	88
No	9	12

said they did not attend worship in the same church as their youth group either come from churches which do not have a youth group, or come from churches which do not have a group where that particular youth feels comfortable attending, or that their parents prefer that they attend elsewhere.

Youth Group Attendance

TABLE 6.14 How long have you been attending your youth group?

YOUTH GROUP ATTENDANCE	MALE (%)	FEMALE (%)
1 year or less	21	20
2 years	20	21
3 years	17	23
4 years	13	14
5 years	9	8
6 years or more	20	13

The youth were asked how long they have attended their youth group. The Tidal Impact youth reported a remarkable loyalty to their youth group. As noted on Table 6.02, 43% of the males and 52% of the females in attendance at Tidal Impact were either 12, 13 or 14 years of age. Thus it would be impossible for about half of the youth attending Tidal Impact to have reported attending their youth group for 4 years or more. In addition, if Tidal Impact youth are generally representative of the Canadian population, one can assume that a significant number of them do not live in the same locale from the time they are 12 until they are 18, given the fact that Statistics Canada (*www.statscan.ca*) reports that 14.3% of Canadians moved in 2001 alone. Thus when the youth report, according to Table 6.14, that 42% of the males and 35% of the females have attended their youth group for 4 years or more, they are making a remarkable statement about loyalty to their youth group.

This loyalty may suggest that the quality of the youth programs is strong in the local churches and that in a secularizing culture Christian youth find support for their faith through their youth groups. The greater likelihood of males having attended their youth group for 4 years or more is probably explained by the fact that, as noted in Table 6.02, the males were generally older than the females.

Baptism

The youth were asked whether they have been baptized, and were given instructions to check as many boxes as applied. The vast majority of the youth (82% of both males and females) who attended Tidal Impact indicated that they had been baptized. This percentage is much higher than the 75% baptism rate reported by the youth attending the 2002 Springforth youth conference (Fawcett and Linkletter, 2003). As might be expected at an event that was mainly comprised of youth from Baptist churches, most stated that they had been baptized either as a child or as a teenager. A surprising number of the youth stated that they had been baptized as a baby (20% male, 26% female) given the fact that very few of the youth attending Tidal Impact, according to Table 6.09, indicated that they were from youth groups representing denominations that engaged in the practice of infant baptism. This suggests that a significant minority of youth in Baptist youth groups were born into families who, at the time of their birth, had their primary religious affiliation with denominations that practice infant baptism such as churches from the Roman Catholic, Anglican, or Presbyterian tradition. It appears likely that due to the existence of very few youth groups in these traditions in Atlantic Canada, some teenagers and/or their families who have an interest in a church youth group experience migrate to some Baptist churches.

TABLE 6.15 Have you been baptized?

BAPTISM	MALE (%)	FEMALE (%)
Yes, as a baby	20	26
Yes, as a child	33	32
Yes, as a teenager	36	36
Yes, as an adult	1	0
No	18	18

In spite of the fact that the vast majority of these highly dedicated youth indicated that they had been baptized, still a significant minority had not been baptized. This suggests that youth leaders need to communicate the importance of Christian baptism to their youth who have made a personal commitment to Christ. Studies have shown (Fawcett and Linkletter, 2003) that youth who have been baptized are more likely to read the scriptures, attend worship more frequently and pray more frequently. Baptism makes a difference in the spiritual commitment level of youth and ought to be encouraged by youth leaders.

¶ Private Religious Practices

Prayer frequency

Respondents were asked if they prayed by themselves. The youth reported frequent involvement in the spiritual discipline of prayer. The data demonstrated that 59% of males and 69% of females indicated that they prayed "Nearly every day." Again, this rate of response was considerably higher than the Grade 9–12 youth surveyed three months earlier at the Springforth youth conference, where only 59% of the youth reported praying nearly every day (Fawcett and Linkletter, 2003).

TABLE 6.16 Do you pray by yourself?

PRAYER FREQUENCY	MALE (%)	FEMALE (%)
Nearly every day	59	69
At least once a week	22	18
At least once a month	5	4
Occasionally	12	8
Never	2	1

Bible reading frequency

The Tidal Impact youth were asked how frequently they read their Bible. The youth reported that they are much less likely to read their Bible than to pray. The data demonstrated that only 44% of males and 53% of females reported reading their Bible "Nearly every day" or "At least once a week." Females were more likely than males to read their Bible frequently, perhaps reflecting their greater interest in, or success with, academics as noted in Table 6.05. Perhaps a lack of modelling, clear teaching from youth leaders about the importance of Bible reading, or lack of encouragement at home may explain the infrequent Bible reading by the youth. It is also possible that with the prevalence of television, video games and other common video-based technology that many teenagers simply do not read anything very often.

TABLE 6.17 Do you read the Bible by yourself?

BIBLE READING FREQUENCY	MALE (%)	FEMALE (%)
Nearly every day	16	23
At least once a week	28	30
At lease once a month	17	14
Occasionally	29	28
Never	10	5

¶ Conclusion

In this chapter it was noted that the youth who attended Tidal Impact are primarily young, teenage females who live on Canada's east coast. Few of these youth have experienced the pain of their parents divorcing. When it comes to schooling, these youth are likely to be top performers who demonstrate a higher interest in French immersion programs than the general population. Concerning their religious background, it has been noted that their fathers and mothers are likely to attend worship weekly. When it comes to public religious practice, these primarily Baptist youth are likely to be baptized. They also tend to be long-term attendees of their church youth group and be active in the public worship of the church where they faithfully attend youth group. Their youth group, which is equally likely to be located in an urban/suburban area or in a small town/village/rural area, tends to be overseen by a paid youth pastor. Finally, regarding private spiritual practices, these youth are highly likely to engage in private prayer and Bible reading.

The youth attending Tidal Impact are very impressive in several ways. First, they are academically able. Second, their enthusiasm for their faith is clear as exhibited by their commitment to public and private religious practices. Finally, the simple fact that they would give up a week of their summer vacation and pay to be involved in service to others is in itself commendable. The churches that commissioned these youth and the parents who raised them can be proud of the selfless nature of these able and committed young people.

¶ References

Fawcett, B. (2000). Effective youth ministry in Atlantic Canada. *Atlantic Baptist*. Summer 2000, 12–17.

Fawcett, B. and Linkletter, J. (2003). *Baptist Youth in Atlantic Canada: how committed are they?* in Bruce Fawcett and Rob Nylen (eds.) (2003) *Effective Youth Ministry* Saint John, New Brunswick, Convention of Atlantic Baptist Churches.

Fawcett, B. and McDonald, M. (2001). *Youth Mission Tours.* Saint John, New Brunswick, United Baptist Convention of the Atlantic Provinces.

Gardner, H. (ed.) (2002). *Yearbook of the Convention of Atlantic Baptist Churches*. Saint John, New Brunswick, Convention of Atlantic Baptist Churches.

7 Preparing Teenagers for Mission

Bruce Fawcett

There are two chief ways to prepare teenagers to go on a mission tour. All churches need to provide "Trip Preparation" for the tasks their students are to undertake on their mission trip. This type of preparation usually involves several training meetings in the month or two leading up to the mission trip where teenagers practice the ministry tasks they will undertake on their trip.

An increasing number of churches are also investing energy and time in "Life Preparation." This type of training involves an extended period of challenge and growth through the winter months in the areas of personal spirituality, ministry involvement and study. This chapter will explore both types of preparation.

¶ Trip preparation

This preparation usually involves setting aside several weeknights or a weekend when students can practice their dramas, puppet shows, Bible lessons, mimes, songs or whatever they will be doing on their mission project. Obviously some mission experiences, like a work camp, require much less preparation than others, such as leading a Vacation Bible School. Leaders will have to use their judgment when deciding not only when and where, but also how long training ought to take and what kinds of training are required.

Before the teenagers can practice and prepare, the leaders will need to determine what ministry responsibilities the various teenagers will have on the trip. It is wise for the leaders to begin by making a complete list of all the ministry roles that will need to be filled. Before the leaders decide who performs what task, it is important to give the team members an opportunity to request a certain role if they feel God has gifted them in a certain area. This can be done by simply reading out the various roles at a meeting of your mission tour team one week before the leaders will be meeting to divide up duties. If anyone has a preference you can suggest that he or she speak to a leader before all the leaders get together to discuss the division of duties.

At the first training meeting of the team, the teenagers should be told what ministry assignments they will have on the trip and be given whatever material they will need to study so they can begin their preparations. For instance, if you will be running a Backyard Bible Club on your mission trip, the song leaders should be given a CD of their songs so they can learn them, the Bible study leaders should be given their lessons so they can review them, and the games leaders should be given their game descriptions.

At the next meeting the work begins for the team. At the beginning of the meeting team members should be given some time to practice and review their parts, and then they should "perform" for each other. The Bible study leaders should teach their lessons and the song leaders should lead their teammates in song. At first this may seem awkward for the teenagers, but when forced to practice in front of others they may realize that they did not know the assigned material as well as they thought they did. There will be no time on the trip to practice, so everything must be ready before you leave. Those you will be ministering to deserve your best, so excellence is required. To further increase quality one more level it is good if the teenagers can perform their ministry in front of the children in their home church. Getting real feedback from children can help them adjust their approach to best reach their audience.

It is very important at all meetings to include a significant amount of time for prayer so that the teenagers are reminded that God is Lord of their trip and talents and that they are dependent upon Him for ministry "success." Themes for prayer should include safety, bonding together as a team, faithfulness in preparation, and a request that God might prepare the hearts of those who will receive ministry during the trip. In addition, a brief devotional thought on themes such as self-sacrifice, hard work, giving, or putting the needs of others first, are also important to remind the team members of the ministry focus of the trip.

You can also take time at these training meetings to brief the team members on practical travel issues that are discussed elsewhere in this book such as dress code, appropriate music and billet etiquette.

In the same way that basketball coaches require attendance at practice in order to play, leaders need to require team members to attend all practices and meetings. Teenagers need to be taught that ministry is a high calling and that service in Christ's name demands dedication and thorough preparation.

¶ Life Preparation – The Discipleship Project

There is, however, another strategy for mission preparation to which churches are increasingly turning their attention. This program encourages habits that are intended to foster a life dedicated to mission and ministry. Many churches are increasingly viewing this program as an effective tool for assisting ministry-minded teens to grow in their faith and discover their spiritual gifts. This training is not offered in place of the essential "trip preparation" for the ministries that the teenagers will lead on their mission tour, but rather as "pre-preparation." *The Discipleship Project* is a fairly rigorous training program that teenagers must complete before they are invited to take part in a mission tour. It is easily adapted to both small and large church settings.

Assumptions: *The Discipleship Project* assumes that in order to mature as a disciple of Jesus teenagers need:

a. *To be doing ministry:* The Christian life is a life of service based on the gifts that God has given us. Teenagers need to be given the opportunity to explore their gifts and experience the joy that comes from using them.

b. *To be meeting God each day in a deliberate devotional encounter:* All Christian believers should be challenged and encouraged to deepen their relationship with God by spending time talking to Him and listening to Him.

c. *To memorize God's Word:* Most Christians do not know the scriptures as well as they think they do. We need to be challenged to memorize and study a brief portion of scripture that we fully and completely digest. God can use this portion of scripture when we face times of trouble or opportunities to witness to our faith.

d. *Opportunities to take responsibility for their own spiritual growth:* My church is not responsible for my spiritual growth ... I am. At a young age all believers need to be challenged to take responsibility for the state of their relationship with God and not to depend on their church or their family to spoon-feed their growth.

e. *Accountability and encouragement from a mentor to accomplish the above:* While the characteristics of a healthy disciple listed above are important, they also do not come easily to most people. It is helpful if each teenager can be assigned a mentor to assist in the process of developing these spiritual disciplines (see Appendix 1 for a mentor's job description).

Key elements: *The Discipleship Project* generally contains (see Appendix 2 for complete curriculum):

a. *A trial month, allowing students to explore the project:* While a four or five month project may not seem like a large commitment to an adult, to a teenager it can seem like a very long time. It is very helpful to provide students with the opportunity to try out the project before asking them to commit to the total package (see Appendix 3 for a sample trial month).

b. *Required daily Bible reading, using a supplied devotional guide:* Students cannot be cast adrift devotionally. You need to provide them with a guide they can use. Some churches have used *Soul Journey*, which is inexpensively distributed in bulk by Radio Bible Class (*www.rbc.org*). This resource can also be sent to your students via email or they can read it online.

c. *Required memorization:* Memorizing about one verse a week with students being required to quote their verses from memory about every eight weeks before moving on to a new set.

d. *Weekly meeting:* Students should have a weekly meeting (biweekly for high school students) with an assigned adult mentor for support, accountability and encouragement.

e. *Ministry projects:* There should be a list of ministry projects from which students can choose and collect a certain number of required points based on time commitment and degree of difficulty.

f. *Electives:* Provide a list of elective options designed for personal learning and growth from which students choose opportunities that coincide with their interests.

Rewards: Some students sign up for the project (see Appendix 4 for a sample sign-up form) because of the rewards attached to the program. Sometimes they see the pure spiritual growth value that comes from being involved in things like ministry projects, Bible study, and scripture memory. Often more tangible types of rewards also attract students. Typical rewards, besides an invitation to take part in the summer mission tour, often include some or all of the following: an invitation to take part in a spring weekend fun trip, subsidized attendance at a local Christian camp's summer counsellor training program and subsidized attendance at Springforth. Another common reward is a Sunday morning recognition service for those who complete the project.

Potential pitfalls: *The Discipleship Project* is not a perfect program and brings with it some risks that every leader ought to carefully consider before implementing such a project:

a. *The wedge:* Some youth group members who do not join the project may feel alienated or distant from the rest of the group as a result of their decision. If this situation is not managed well it could result in the creation of factions within your ministry.

b. *Equating spirituality with the project and its assignments:* Completing assignments does not ensure a vibrant spiritual life.

c. *Late arrivals:* Some students will arrive after you have already started the project and may wish to join. You will need to handle this issue carefully by both preserving the integrity of the project and honouring the hard work that the other teenagers have done, without shutting out those who wish to grow in their faith.

d. *Children of key church leaders may not finish the project:* As a leader you would like to think that other church leaders could be mature and see the advantages for the group, even if their own teenager withdraws from the project, thus ruling out participation in the mission project. However, if this scenario develops, it will be awkward and difficult. Be prepared for possible friction.

e. *Money:* Some board members who don't understand the vision may balk at the idea of subsidizing the cost for teens to be part of special life-changing events.

f. *Changing the rules for mission project participation:* If mission tours have taken place without *The Discipleship Project* as a requirement, you can expect some level of resistance from the students to all the work that you are proposing.

g. *Creating a lot of work for yourself:* The benefits of *The Discipleship Project* are many, and you may need to expand your leadership team so that you can add this type of growth opportunity to your youth ministry (see Appendix 5 for the coordinator's job description).

Side benefits: In addition to risks that are not evident at first, the project also can have some important side benefits that are not immediately apparent.

a. *Death to the "One-eared Mickey Mouse"*: Local church youth ministry can exist much like a loose appendage to the body, attached only in name, not interacting with the wider body. Deliberate or unintentional age segregation is common to such an extent that in many churches, especially larger churches, some teenagers very rarely interact with adults. This means that teens often have no appreciation for the wider ministry of the church or see that they have a role in giving as well as receiving ministry to the wider body. *The Discipleship Project* can help address this problem.

b. *Many mentors:* Most of us who are youth leaders are very conscious of our own shortcomings and spiritual failings. Some of us have found ourselves awake late at night pleading with God not to let the teens in our charge develop the same weaknesses we possess. By having several different mentors during one's youth group experience, teens can see the Christian faith lived out at many stages of life by people in different life situations. This can help teens see more fully how Christian faith can be integrated into their life.

c. *Ministry support:* Involving many adults in the ministry assists the youth ministry point person in building support for the ministry. The more people from within your church that are involved in the church's youth ministry, the greater the prayer and financial support.

d. *Extra workers for church programs:* Allowing teens to serve as junior leaders or leaders-in-training with church programs may allow some adult leaders to be redeployed into other areas of service. Whereas two leaders were needed in a classroom, now perhaps one adult and one teen would suffice.

e. *Long-term integration:* A teenager who is involved in *The Discipleship Project* for several years will have had several mentors and will have served alongside countless adults in ministry, thus ensuring contact with many Christian adults. This can ease integration into the wider life of the church following high school graduation.

f. *Increased marketability for teens for summer mission and Christian camp opportunities:* All leaders want their teenagers to have the opportunity to grow through further involvement in ministry. Students who have completed a program like *The Discipleship Project* will more likely gain the desire for further involvement in ministry and possess greater skills and maturity than their peers.

g. *Retention:* Teens who are going through a rough time may not be as quick to bail from your youth ministry if they are intrigued by trips and other rewards.

h. *Growth in numbers:* A few years after the program gets established, if the mission tours and other rewards are well received, teens will likely bring their friends.

i. *Defining normalcy:* You have the opportunity to create in young lives the clear understanding that the normal Christian life involves service, personal Bible reading and scripture memory.

j. *You will, in time, gain quality adult leaders for your church:* While it is not a short term fix to the leadership crunch you may be experiencing now in your church, some teenagers who complete this project will likely remain in your area after high school graduation, eventually resulting in more capable leaders than you would have had without the project.

k. *You will have a rationale for what teens you spend time with:* One of the most important ministry principles for leaders to remember is to spend time with those who want to grow. Involvement in this project is a sure sign that teenagers wish to grow, thus those who commit to the project deserve your time.

l. *Only teens that are ready will go on your mission tour:* Many leaders have found themselves in the awkward situation of trying to discourage a student who lacks the personal or spiritual maturity from going on a mission tour. By requiring completion of *The Discipleship Project* to participate in the trip, leaders have created a winnowing process that usually means only qualified students go on the trip.

m. *You will develop a network of adults from which you can recruit leaders for other youth ministries:* Mentors who have a positive experience with teenagers make likely future youth leaders.

Typical first year struggles: The addition of any new program is usually hardest in the first year. Here are some common struggles that people face in the first year of incorporating *The Discipleship Project* into their youth ministry.

a. *Making the project too hard and causing the teens to become discouraged:* The first year we offered this program at Lewisville Baptist Church in Moncton, New Brunswick, I made the great mistake of requiring the memorization of 48 verses. That was too many. For many participants, all they could see was the scripture memory and not the rest of the project. We had many quit and we did not experience the results we had hoped.

b. *Not explaining the rationale for the project to the teens, thus ensuring grumbling and complaining about hard work:* Like adults, teenagers need to understand the rationale for any change. If they are accustomed to going on a mission experience with little advanced preparation being required, you will need to carefully explain to them why completing this project is important and in their best interests.

c. *Not giving proper supervision to teens:* Some leaders have assumed that you can just wind up this project and let it go. The coordinator of the project will need to carefully monitor each teenager's progress through regular phone calls and personal conversations. Do not leave it all up to the mentors.

d. *Mentors who lack clarity in their responsibilities and importance:* It is important to provide a job description and a little training for the mentors so they understand their role and how important they are to a teenager successfully completing the program.

e. *Having someone in charge of the program who lacks administrative ability and follow through:* Sometimes the problem is us! Not all youth leaders are gifted administratively. In order for this project to be successful, a lot of administrative labor is required. It may be best to appoint someone else as the coordinator and for you to serve as the "champion" for the project.

f. *Shortage of mentors because those you would ask are probably already heavily involved in church life:* While serving as an advisor in the project does not take a lot of time, it is still a new layer of service that you are asking people to take on for a season. It may be best to ask people far in advance if they are willing to serve in this capacity rather than spring it on them at the last minute and hope for enough positive responses so that the program can go ahead.

¶ Trouble Shooting

Some students will not complete the project. Perhaps they never signed up. Perhaps they dropped out part way through. What do you do with these students? Normally, to maintain your personal credibility and to honour the hard work of those who complete the project, it is important to stick to the rules you set out at the beginning. Those who do not finish generally cannot be invited to go on the trip. But what about occasions when someone does not complete the project and you really feel they should go on the mission trip anyway? Mike McDonald tells me that he deals with this concern by telling the youth who sign up for the project that it may be the case that an "unusual situation" develops during the life of the project. Perhaps someone new joins the group or someone who did not sign up has a Christian conversion experience and wants to be part of the mission team. Mike then explains to those who sign up that in the event of an unusual development he reserves the right to meet with them as a group, explain the situation and then ask them to vote on allowing this individual to join the mission team. Mike's experience is that an "unusual situation" develops almost every year and that he has yet the see the team vote against including someone whose case he pleads.

It is important to stress for students who choose to withdraw or not to participate that they can always join next year. It is also important to maintain contact with them and invite them to other events. You might want to invite them to be part of the prayer team for those going on the trip so they have a role in the mission tour.

Sticking to the rules will be very difficult but you need to remember that the long-term benefits can outweigh the difficulties. You are trying to create a new culture in your youth ministry that stresses powerful themes that can result in personal as well as local church renewal and growth.

¶ Conclusion

The Discipleship Project can be a great benefit to your church's youth ministry. At Lewisville Baptist Church it was an engine that helped to drive the spiritual and numerical growth of our ministry for years. Dozens of other churches have adapted it and made it work for them. It can allow your teenagers new avenue for growth. It can give you a better-prepared mission team than you have ever had and it can help to focus your ministry on some very important themes. To make it fly, simply present it as a one-year experiment, adapt it carefully to your church, make the trips fantastic and work very hard at retention in the first year. This kind of general preparation offered alongside specific preparation can result in a well-prepared and confident team who approach their mission tour not only with energy and enthusiasm, but also with a fairly well developed understanding of their giftedness and talents.

8 Budgeting & Administrative Details

Mike McDonald

It's important to be able to outline for your boards, your participants and their parents, how much the mission tour is going to cost and the rationale for the costs. Always have a parents meeting before the trip, handing out cost break-downs and estimates to show how all of the hard earned funds will be spent. There is always a great deal of appreciation for this and I've had parents throw additional funds into the overall account to make sure that the group has more than enough money to make the trip happen. The parents should have been aware of the trip months in advance, with a permission form and accompanying explanation letter being sent home with the youth. In Appendix 8, you can see how a payment schedule may also be incorporated into your registration form, as well as using one form for two mission tours. This form has worked extremely well for our group.

Safety: Safety is a huge issue, so showing line items for insurances and documentation of the coverage is also important. Be sure to purchase the maximum amount of insurance coverage for the teens and leaders riding in the vans, or obtain the best possible travel insurance coverage if you're heading out of the country. In recent years, it's been necessary to call the church insurance carrier and ask them to fax a copy of the church insurance coverage with a rider added to it. The rider should indicate every location in which you are going to be conducting your ministry. For example, for our puppet ministry it named the ferry boats and ferry terminals, and the full names and addresses of every mall and school, as well as the anticipated dates. While there might be an additional expense involved, at the time of writing this I have yet to incur any extra costs.

Letters of excuse: In advance, make up letters to excuse participants from classes, lessons, employment or anything they might miss at home as a result of the trip. I've led numerous trips to Newfoundland on the Victoria Day weekend in May. This has resulted in youth missing a day or two from school. Parents, teachers and principals have always been supportive of the trips when they see excuse notes in advance. Make photocopies of a generic letter for everyone whereby only the name of the participant needs to be filled in at the top. At the bottom of the letter I make a point of telling the recipient to contact me if they have any questions regarding the authenticity of the letter.

Keeping track of money: During the mission tour make sure you obtain all receipts and keep track of your expenditures in a notebook as you travel. You can start with an opening balance and keep a running tally of what you have left. This way, you can pace yourselves in your spending and should always know if you have a bit of a surplus for ice cream or other special treats on the last day.

When you arrive home, add up all the receipts and compare the expenditures against the person who kept the running tally. You can also compare your actual expenses against your budget. Then submit a final report to the church treasurer, making sure that the parents receive a final report along with their receipts for their contributions.

¶ Establishing a budget

Establishing the budget is probably the most difficult part of administrating a mission tour. Over the next few pages we will look at some actual budgets on different types of trips, for the following reasons:

- To be able to derive best possible estimates on trip costs
- To show how to develop a break-even analysis based on number of participants
- To offer examples of different types of trips and expenditures involved
- To compare budget amounts to actual amounts spent so that you learn from your own efforts and become progressively better at budgeting

Estimating trip costs: First, break down your expected costs into major categories. I always start with different modes of travel. I might have van costs in one section with ferryboat or air fares in a separate section. You can calculate the cost of gasoline or diesel fuel with the van rental costs. The next major category would be food, then lodging, then conference costs, followed by sightseeing or amusement costs and finally a miscellaneous category.

Starting with the van costs, phone all of the rental agencies in the area and get the best price on the vehicles you have in mind. Usually, one 15-passenger van is much cheaper than two mini-vans, whether they are seven or eight seat vans. The more recent problem is that fewer rental places are now carrying the bigger vans. Begin to establish a cost based on daily or weekly rental rates, insurances, mileage costs and fuel consumption. Most new car dealers have guides that will tell you what fuel ratings to expect on all vehicles.

The next thing to do is calculate your mileage. You can either use a road map which usually has a chart with mileage between major cities, or you can go on-line to a website that will calculate this for you. I prefer to use *www.mapblast.com* as it will also provide maps and driving directions. You enter your church address and address of your final destination and the rest is calculated for you. Keep in mind that you might have to calculate this search in segments, as going from Halifax to Toronto might calculate your route through the United States, rather than Quebec. If you want to stay in Canada, go from Halifax to Rivière-du-Loup, Québec, then on to Toronto.

Once you get the mileage in one direction, double it, and then add in any estimated driving around at your destination. You might calculate a 1400 km drive to Toronto, plus the same for the return trip, and then 100 km a day for 5 days while you are in Toronto. Your total would be 1400 km × 2 trips = 2800 km to get there and back, plus 5 days x 100 km/day = 500 km while you are there, for a total of 3300 km. If the rental company is allowing you 100 free kilometres per day for 9 days, then you subtract this 900 km from 3300 km and pay for the additional 2400 km. If the rate is 18 cents per kilometre, mileage alone will cost you $432.00 plus tax. I usually add an extra ten percent to these mileage estimates, just to be safe.

Once I arrive at a total cost for the van rental and gas, then I divide that by the number of people occupying seats in the vans. This is where it gets tricky, as empty seats cost everyone extra money and makes budgeting difficult. This is where I develop a break-even analysis. Using break-even figures from my trip to Newfoundland in 2003, you can see the difference in costs based on number of participants. In this analysis, you can also see where I have added toll costs in with the van figures and even showed zeros if we got a special deal on tolls or used a borrowed vehicle. Although I can't divulge how I managed to get some of these special deals, if you know the right people and ask for special discounts for the youth in your group, most people are more than willing to see what they can do to help.

You can also see where I factored in the cost of our registrations at the retreat, team t-shirts, and food. Food can be calculated at a per person cost per day (for example, breakfast $5, lunch $10 and supper $15 = $30 per person per day). Costs seem to go up each year, however, going from Prince Edward Island to Newfoundland and Labrador, this was a fairly inexpensive week away. If you don't have church budget or any other extra funds to fall back on, you might want to consider adding a small cushion or miscellaneous line item to cover any unforeseen expenses.

Break-Even Analysis

YOUTH MISSION TOUR TO NEWFOUNDLAND, MAY 2003 **(based on 23 people with one rental van)**		
15-passenger van	rental charge for 1 week	$360.00
	3000 km. – 700 km. free = 2300 km. × $0.10 =	$230.00
	GST	$ 41.30
	Collision Protection Charge (with PST)	$128.40
	PST	$ 63.13
		$822.83
8-passenger Suburban (borrowed – FREE)		0.00
Northumberland Ferries (off PEI – FREE)		0.00
Cobequid Pass tolls ($3.50 × 2 vehicles)		$7.00
Gas for both vehicles	Safe estimate based on past trips with these 2 vehicles (400 liters × .813 cents/liter PEI & Nfld – NS is lower)	$650.40
Marine Atlantic Ferry (to NFLD)	Vans – $72.75 × 2 vehicles × 2 crossings (tax included)	$291.00
	Passengers – $25.00 × 23 people x 2 crossings (tax included)	$1150.00
	Dormitory Sleepers – $16.75 × 23 people ($14.50+ HST)	$383.53
	Cabin (return trip) $46.00 ($40 + HST)	$46.00
Mission Tour T-shirts	$9.50 each × 23 =$218.50 + $21.85 PST =	$240.35
Charge for Retreat at Twin Ponds Camp	$85/person × 23 people =	$1955.00
Food	Meals while travelling. Based on past trips $40/person × 23 people =	$920.00
	Grand total	$6466.11
	Per person costs (23 people)	**$281.14**

YOUTH MISSION TOUR TO NEWFOUNDLAND, MAY 2003 (based on 27 people with two rental vans)		
15-passenger van	rental charge for 1 week	$360.00
	3000 km. – 700 km. free = 2300 km. × $0.10	$230.00
	GST	$41.30
	Collision Protection Charge (with PST)	$128.40
	PST	$63.13
		$822.83
		× 2 vans
		$1645.66
Northumberland Ferries (off PEI)	FREE	$0.00
Cobequid Pass tolls:	$3.50 × 2 vehicles =	$7.00
Gas for both vehicles:	Safe estimate based on past trips with these 2 vehicles (800 liters × .813 cents/liter PEI & Nfld – NS is lower)	$650.40
Marine Atlantic Ferry (to NFLD)	Vans – $72.75 × 2 vehicles x 2 crossings (tax included)	$291.00
	Passengers – $25.00 × 27 people × 2 crossings (tax included)	$1350.00
	Dormitory Sleepers – $16.75 × 27 people ($14.50 + HST)	$450.23
	Cabin (return trip) $46.00 ($40 + HST)	$46.00
Mission Tour T-shirts	$9.50 each × 27 = $256.50 + $25.65 PST =	$282.15
Charge for Retreat at Twin Ponds Camp	$85/person × 27 people =	$2295.00
Food	(meals while travelling, based on past trips) $40/person x 27 people =	$1080.00
	Grand total	$8097.44
	Per person (27 people)	$299.91

As you can see, the cost of this trip varies somewhat based on the number of people going and the vehicles used. By the time we had our parents meeting to discuss the budget, we had decided to take two 15-passenger rental vans. We had twenty-three people signed up, anticipated adding two more, but due to illness, only twenty-two people went. When we told the parents that we were keeping the trip at a cost of $300 per person and the church budget would handle the difference, some parents and church leaders came forward and helped us with extra funds. During the trip, we saved money on food and fuel, and came in at $301 per person.

¶ Different Trips and Expenditures Involved

The following (see next page) is the budget for a large-group trip to Hong Kong in 2003. Unfortunately, the trip was cancelled due to the outbreak of SARS and travel advisories by the World Health Organization.

Unusual items to consider in this budget were exchange rates with three different currencies, costs before departure for a team meeting and administration fees. These fees covered costs for photocopying, postage and phone calls, considering we had 43 people from Atlantic Canada in this group, 4 from Toronto, 2 from Texas and 8 from Australia. Our figures were for the Canadian team members. We also had excluded costs for passports, optional vaccinations, team Canada hats, extra travel insurance and of course, spending money. In the end, the SARS epidemic drove airline costs much higher and we would have had to come up with those funds or forfeit down payments. As it was, each team member lost their $100 deposit with the travel agent and nothing else. All of these costs and the resulting cancellation were out of the ordinary.

Greg Pike, pastor of Corner Brook Baptist Church assisted me with the details of planning for this trip. He had the largest number of church members within this group of 58 people, including himself and three out of five of his own children. Greg makes the

HONG KONG BUDGET (As of March 12, 2003)		
Airfare	Northwest: Halifax to Detroit to Tokyo to Hong Kong	$1781.00
Royal Insurance	Adult Price; $34.00 for youth under 30	$42.00
Conference	1 USD = 1.47557 CAD as of March 12, 2003	$184.45
Team Meeting	Training & Lunch – Moncton, Feb. 22, 2003	$15.00
Camp & Meals	1982 HKD ÷ 5.28510 exchange rate as of March 12, 2003	$375.02
Other Meals	($10 × 7 Suppers) + ($5 × 7 lunches)	$105.00
Local Travel	$60.00 ferry to Macau	$144.94
	Octopus Card ($2/trip x twice/day × 15 days)	$60.00
	Airport Bus (airport to camp – camp to airport)	$22.94
Miscellaneous	Est. Exchange rate fluctuation on US and HK dollars ($32.59)	
	Admin. Fee (postage, courier, paper, photocopies, devotional booklet ($20.00)	
	Museums/Attractions – subsidy ($50.00)	$102.59
Total	(Adult Price)	**$2750.00**
	(Youth under 30)	**$2742.00**
Excludes	*Passports ($35/$85), Vaccinations (Tetanus/Diphtheria/Polio – $25, Hepatitis A&B $105/$195, Typhoid $40), Roots Canada Hats ($20.25), Extra Travel Insurance and Spending Money.*	

following four observations with regards to budgeting for a mission tour, particularly one of this magnitude. When it comes to mission tours with large budgets which have several sources of income there are four things that are crucial. First, begin early, developing financial plans and raising money. Spread out your fundraising, with the bulk happening the year of your mission trip. Second, try to keep the plan as simple as possible. Third, no matter how simple you think the plan is, never assume that everyone understands the procedures after one or two explanations. Fourth, with big budgets, money is often given to the church and said money is legally not allowed to be refunded, therefore you must do two things. Keep as much of the donations in a bank account until the last moment and then give it over to the church. In addition, make sure there is a clear understanding of what will happen to any money which has been given to the church and which is not used by the mission tour due to trip cancellation or simply left over funds.

It is important for everyone's integrity, that if designated donated money is not used due to the trip being cancelled, the money be held until another similar mission trip is planned and not spent on other youth events. People have given that money for missions and their wishes must be honoured even if it takes another few years.

¶ Comparing Budget to Actual Costs

Once a mission tour is over, establish a chart showing budgeted figures versus actual expenses. Keep these figures around for when you budget in future years and you will not only learn from your mistakes, but also take less time in recalculating the costs. The following (see next page) is a good example.

In this example, you can see that we only overspent by $1.45 per person. During the trip, I recognized that tolls, the ferryboat and swimming pool rental were fixed costs. When we picked up the 15-passenger van the morning of departure, we found out at that time that it used diesel fuel. Diesel was considerably lower in price at the time, so I knew we would save on fuel. Watching the mileage and having done the trip before, I drove 2970 kilometres instead of the 3000 that I budgeted, so we experienced a small savings there. The people at the camp were good enough to give us two free registrations, considering we had travelled the furthest distance and also boosted their overall attendance. In other words, our presence created a surplus of funds for them which they shared with us, so we saved more money. All of this allowed us to splurge a little on meals, ice cream and other goodies and miscellaneous items.

YOUTH MISSION TOUR TO NEWFOUNDLAND, MAY 2004
(based on 22 people with one rental van)

	BUDGET	ACTUAL	
15-passenger van	$1269.13	$1262.75	
8-passenger Van (borrowed – FREE)	0.00	0.00	
Professionally Clean 8-passenger Van	$69.00	$28.69	*(Opted for Oil Change instead)*
Tolls	$16.00	16.00	
Gas for both vehicles	$767.20	696.58	*(15-Passenger used diesel)*
Marine Atlantic Ferry	$1895.60	$1895.60	
Retreat/Camp at $85/ person × 22 people	$1870.00	1700.00	*(the camp allowed 2 free!)*
Swimming Pool Rental	$40.25	$40.25	
Miscellaneous (Ice, Payphones, Parking, etc.)	$14.00	$52.58	
Food at $35/person × 22 people	$770.00	$1050.65	
Total	$6711.18	$6743.10	
Per Person Cost (22 people)	$305.05	$306.50	

Knowing our limits, we stayed very close to our original budget. However, knowing where I saved and not expecting to experience that saving every time, I would probably budget $330 to $350 per person if I were to repeat this trip the next year. The first time I took a group of teens on this particular trip in 1999, the cost was $250 per person, but the trip was one day shorter. Budgets constantly fluctuate and it's always easier to give extra money back rather than try to collect more funds after the trip is over.

¶ Final reminder

While I cannot divulge all of my sources for savings along the way, let me encourage you in two areas. First, if you're going to save money, it's because of the relationships you build with the people that you encounter during your planning and participating in mission tours. Second, (even though grammatically incorrect) I always say "if you don't ask, you don't get" (Jesus said "ask and you shall receive"). The worst anyone can say to you when you ask is "no." Personally, I never hesitate to ask for a deal or a break when it's for the youth in my group. They stand to reap the eternal benefits of the entire mission tour and most people recognize this when they pass along the savings to your group.

¶ Conclusion

A fine-tuned budget can allow you to determine the amount of money you charge those participating in your mission tour. It also communicates to your board and your parents that you have carefully thought through the nature of your trip and the expenses associated with it. Careful documentation and proper reporting will preserve you and your leaders from any accusations of mismanagement or carelessness with other people's funds. While for many, the budgeting process is taxing, it is a necessary ingredient to a well planned mission tour.

9 Financing Your Trip

Mike McDonald

Financial concerns can make or break your proposal to take a group of young people on a mission tour. Veteran youth leaders report that the number one concern expressed by parents when presented with a mission tour idea is "How much will this cost?" Thus as a leader your approach to financing your project is very important. Introducing some solid fundraising principles during early planning stages will help determine the success of your proposed trip. There are four principles that must be considered and then four courses of action that may be taken.

❡ Principles

Ministry and money: First and foremost, remember to adopt a spiritual perspective towards the financing of any project: "The ministry dictates the money, the money does not dictate the ministry." If the undertaking is of God, He will make sure that the funds are there for the project to happen. We are to do His will and let Him do the worrying about how things will be paid for. Our faith will grow as we see God coming alongside our efforts. We still have a role to play but we need ultimately to trust God for the results.

Sharing everything: Remind your team of the events that took place in Acts 4:32–36:

> *All the believers were one in heart and mind. No one claimed that any of his possessions was his own, but they shared everything they had. With great power the apostles continued to testify to the resurrection of the Lord Jesus, and much grace was upon*

them all. There were no needy persons among them. For from time to time those who owned lands or houses sold them, brought the money from the sales and put it at the apostles' feet, and it was distributed to anyone as he had need. Joseph, a Levite from Cyprus, whom the apostles called Barnabas (which means Son of Encouragement), sold a field he owned and brought the money and put it at the apostles' feet.

The principle in this story is community building. Leaders and teens need to learn to share with one another if they are truly going to become a team of Christians who are going out to do the work that the Lord has called them to do. The teens usually embrace this idea much easier than their parents. Many times I have witnessed teens being willing to give extra money from their fundraising effort to another teen who would not have been able to go on the trip without this help. Parents don't always agree with giving money away so freely, but do so at their child's request. It's great when the youth teach their parents.

Handling funds: You should separate the money from the youth pastor or leader to create as much distance as possible between their position and the funds. Pastors and leaders are there to pastor and to lead, not to be accountants. There are a lot of people in the congregation who have skills in this area and allowing them to help will reduce the stress load for the pastor. Pastors or youth leaders may wind up going to great lengths accounting for funds, spending precious time generating reports. Learn to give up control of some of these things and empower others who could carry on these duties in your absence. Always try to operate as though you might not be there tomorrow and others will need to carry on the vision.

Don't take this principle too lightly. In the days of professional leaders being called into question for so many different things, find some lay people who need to exercise the gifts that God has given to them. A good way to do this is to form a committee or board of finance from parents, leaders and members with talents in handling and investing funds. This committee should have at least three people. Any one of the three can collect and deposit the funds into a bank account, while cheques should require signatures of any two of the three. This keeps everyone accountable, making sure no one is called into question. The committee can determine who will make deposits and who will make payments. Someone might also be asked to invest funds on hand. Putting your funds into short-term guaranteed investments will help to earn interest. Even having your funds in a savings account will earn a little bit of interest for you, as in the parable of the talents (Matthew 25:27). If your church treasurer will look after a lot of this for you, don't look a gift horse in the mouth. This might mean that you cannot invest the funds, but it might be worth it to have the church treasurer doing this work for your group.

Giving to Caesar, and God: Finally, remember that Jesus said: "Give to Caesar what is Caesar's, and to God what is God's" (Matthew 22: 21). This applies to the funds that are raised by your group. Give to the government what is rightfully owed them. There are laws dictating what your group must pay taxes on if you are buying items to sell. You don't necessarily have to charge the tax to others when you are selling items or offering services, depending on your particular circumstances. It is best to call the toll-free numbers in the white pages of your phone book to find out from the federal government what your responsibilities are with regards to taxes. Some taxes that you pay might be reclaimed through different rebates. Your church should have a number showing your registration as a charity with the federal government. You will need to know this number when dealing with tax issues. With regards to giving to God what is God's, it is a good idea to challenge your group to tithe from the funds that they earn. It teaches them good biblical principles and helps them to look beyond their own needs while expanding their faith even further.

¶ Courses of Action

Based on these principles, you need to decide what approach you want to take in obtaining funds for a mission tour. There are basically four schools of thought and you may pick one to use exclusively, or some combination of any or all four. They are as follows:

- Teens and their families pay their own way
- Budget for the trip within the operating budget of the church
- Make special appeals for donations
- Fundraise

There are advantages and disadvantages to all four of these approaches. Some individuals or churches may only be comfortable with one or two of these approaches, so be careful to find out what sort of ground you are standing on before you proceed.

Teens and families pay their own way: This approach is no different then most school trips. The cost is determined, parents and teens are told what the cost is and a payment schedule is set up to allow the trip to be paid for over the course of a few months or a year. This approach is very easy for the youth leader to implement. Fifty or a hundred dollars at a time is a lot easier to take for most people than paying for the whole trip at once. Teens contribute from their part-time jobs or allowance. Parents or grandparents might also contribute depending on the circumstances, values and resources within each family. Even though the money goes into one account for the trip, separate records must be kept for the contributions of each participant. The downside of this approach is there is a decreased opportunity of sharing funds and teens with little or no funds are left out of the trip.

Budget for the trip within the operating budget of the church: A youth pastor from the west coast had been in Harare, Zimbabwe, with a team of ten teens and leaders. The total cost of the trip was $40,000, which is a staggering figure for most youth groups to fundraise. However, this pastor only had to raise $10,000 of the total cost. The other $30,000 came out of the church budget. This is unheard of in some churches, but there are churches that handle their activities this way. This approach relieves strain from both youth leaders and parents if there is little or no fundraising. The teens are not constantly coming to the church and asking for money for their project if all or most of it is looked after. It relieves a lot of pressure and extra work, which is great for the youth pastor. On the negative side, it takes away a little of the ownership from the teens. To get the most out of a trip you have to do a little work to get there in the first place. That doesn't mean that financing the trip has to take over your life. It just means that teens need to have some responsibility in making the trip happen. If it's just handed to them, chances are you will end up with some teens going who do not really want to go, or who will get little out of the adventure because they had very little in the way of expectations or personal investment. Also, this could create a problem in deciding who gets to go at the expense of the church.

Make special appeals for donations: Sometimes in lieu of budgeting for a project, a church will allow the teens and leaders to make a special appeal to the congregation. This could be during a specific Sunday morning worship service or during a number of Sundays over a period of time leading up to the trip. The teens will usually take part in the leadership of the service and the trip will be explained in detail with regards to purpose, destination and costs. Funds on hand may be compared with total amounts needed and the congregation can be encouraged to make donations which they can write off against their own personal income taxes. Sometimes this works very well. At other times the response can be very discouraging. It's hard to say why these efforts work better at some times than others. The important thing is that you are getting the message out to the congregation regarding what you are doing with the teens. If they think it is worthwhile, they will help if they are able to.

In one instance we had raised half of the money we needed towards a goal of $20,000 for our trip. A member of the church told me that he would write a cheque for the difference when it came time to go on the trip. We had appealed to the congregation and they had helped as much as they could. This man wanted to remove the stress from me, as pastor, so that I could focus on ministry rather than on fundraising. I had no idea as to his personal finances or his generosity prior to that conversation, and I still don't, but he was serious. He asked me not to share this with the teens or leaders because he wanted them to still work hard for the trip. He knew that working for it would make it more worthwhile to all involved. Four days before departure, I asked him for a cheque for $175.15, which he promptly wrote. He was prepared to write a cheque for $10,000, which thankfully he didn't have to do. But he had relieved my stress and given me the confidence to share with the rest of the group my belief that the Lord would indeed provide for the trip. There are a lot of good folks in the world like this one man and they are a blessing to you and your ministry when you allow them to help out.

Fundraise: These can be the worst two syllables ever uttered to a group of parents. The schools, bands, sports teams and choirs all fundraise. Parents don't want any more of this than they have to experience, but if it means allowing their son or daughter to go on a worthwhile trip, many will do it. It's good for their child to work towards something worthwhile and it removes the financial burden from them. In a lot of cases, the parents will tell stories of fundraising memories from when they were in school and how they want their children to experience the same thing. Remember a few key points:

a. *What works with one church or group does not always work in another church:* Each situation is unique for any number of reasons and something very lucrative for one group may not work in your particular situation. One church had a glow-in-the-dark golf tournament and broke dead even. The little bit of money raised paid for the glow-in-the-dark markers and pins that lit up the golf balls. It was fun, but they earned nothing for their efforts. When a local charity had done the same event in the same town, they made thousands of dollars. They knew the golfers, picked the best time of year and did things a church group wouldn't, such as making use of the bar at the golf course.

b. *Try not to lay out any up front expenses:* The church put out money in advance for the golf event. If it had turned out worse than it did, they would have had to draw the money from some other source to pay for the miscalculation. If you are selling things, get orders ahead of time and order supplies based on demand.

c. *Don't violate basic Christian principles when you fundraise:* What about fundraisers such as lotteries or raffles? People are buying tickets with no guarantee of any return on their investment. This could cause quite a debate within your church. Rather than venturing into the grey area that some people do not consider as gambling, determine that you will always offer something tangible when people spend their money. Avoid making your way down the slippery slope of trying to define what is gambling and what is not.

d. *Do you keep separate accounts for funds raised by each team member or do you set up one giant fund as per the passage from Acts 4:* Do you set up separate accounts or do you set quotas? Do you tell each teen they must sell a certain number of each item or make up the difference out of their own pocket? If you do, there is little difference between this approach and having teens and their families pay their own way for the trip. The teens should be doing the fundraising, not their parents or the youth leaders. There's nothing wrong with having the teens help raise funds for the leaders. If they want to go on the trip, they should be helping the adults who are already giving up their vacation time to participate. Remember to pray through your fundraising choices. God will honour your efforts as long as you continue to honour Him.

e. *How do you market yourself:* Will the church allow you to make announcements on Sunday morning or in the church bulletin or newsletter? Can you display items in the front entrance of the church? What if money changes hands on Sunday morning? It's quite easy to be compared to the money changers thrown out of the temple by Jesus (John 2:13–16). At the same time, remember that the apostle Paul himself was a tentmaker (Acts 18:3). He made and sold tents to finance his missionary efforts.

f. *If you are going to sell a product or a service as a youth group try to pick something that people need:* We always found that people were looking for trees at Christmas and flowers for Mother's Day. People don't really need chocolate bars, although there is nothing stopping you from selling them if it's acceptable to your church leaders.

g. *Finally, make sure that the church board members, the senior pastor and the rest of the staff are in agreement with what you plan to do as a fundraiser:* Remember, other organizations are fundraising as well, and there's nothing worse than doing something that's already been done or is being done. You might have to experiment with what works best for your group. Be sure to seek approval from the senior pastor and church boards before you try something that's never been done at your church. If they are not behind you there might be problems.

¶ Fundraising Ideas

Here are some fundraising activities that have worked well in the past for our groups. Remember, not all of these will work for everyone.

Christmas trees: Knowing a wonderfully generous man who owned a Christmas tree lot on the other side of the province was a blessing to our group. He supplied us with trees at a price very close to his cost, and we added $7 per tree, selling three different grades of trees based on how full they looked. We took orders for two or three weeks, then ordered the trees we needed, plus a few extra for folks that walked up to us on the street. They were available in the church parking lot for pickup. We were never left with extra trees.

Flowers: Poinsettias sell well at Christmas, but they require a lot of care to survive the cold weather. Instead, we sold hanging baskets for Mother's Day, in the same manner in which we sold Christmas trees. The profit margin was about $5 per basket and it was amazing how many of these we would sell. Again, we would take orders ahead of time, and have a few extras on hand. We always had parents in charge of this event who knew a lot about flowers.

Pies: We were able to order pies directly from a company that supplied the local grocery store. With food items, refrigeration is a major concern and the pies must be picked up or delivered in a timely manner. We took advance orders for individual pies or cases of six and limited the choices to no more than six different flavours.

Bird houses: We had a number of nature lovers in our congregation, so we sold bird houses. One man in our congregation bought the lumber and nails and cut out all of the pieces according to a simple blueprint that we found. We sold the assembled birdhouses along with a mounting stick and two screws. Our cost was about $3 per house, and we sold them for $10.

Car washes: This is a great group building activity. It does give you a sense of teamwork and can be fun, but at $5 or $6 per car, it's hard to make a lot of money. You will need to buy some sponges and soap, and come up with a few buckets, hoses, and a large washing area. The paved church parking lot usually works well. You'll also need plenty of sun screen and a few adults to keep all of the teens working. Some groups pre-sell their carwash by soliciting donations from the congregation and washing whatever cars come along on Saturday morning. Don't leave car washes until just before you are going on your trip, because if you are counting on these funds, the weather can cause problems. If it rains, you have to find another Saturday morning as a make up day.

Barbeques: We were able to have a barbeque at our local grocery store. We sold hot dogs, hamburgers, drinks and popsicles, all supplied by the grocer. The store also supplied the grill and propane and enforced cleanliness standards. Many stores are set up for this kind of activity if you inquire. We were set up outside the store where we could catch customers as they were coming and going. Try to hold this on a busy weekend, such as Canada Day and remember you are at the mercy of the weather for good profits. Again, you will need to supply sunscreen and hats for your workers.

Renting the local theatre: We once rented the local theatre with the understanding that we would sell a certain number of tickets before actually being committed to paying the bill. More than one week before the showing we had sold more than enough tickets to break even, so we confirmed our commitment to the theatre. They showed the movie *Shadowlands* which was about the great Christian writer, C. S. Lewis. We made over $500 doing this on a Saturday, even though the show time was at 4:00 p.m., right after the matinee, and before the first evening showing.

Dinners: We have hosted take out dinners, which consisted of ham, potato salad, celery sticks and other goodies in Styrofoam containers at $5 per plate. The meals were picked up or delivered over lunch hour. You could also host a sit down meal of roast turkey or barbeque chicken and pork at the church. Make sure your facility is up to the standards of your local board of health and be careful with things like potato salad that may contain mayonnaise. There is no point in doing a fundraiser which is going to lead to other difficulties for others and yourself.

¶ Conclusion

Finally, with regards to fundraising, we need to realize that not every church has the same view on fundraising. You need to decide upon the best approach to fundraising for your church and then pray through your approach with your team members and the church leadership.

10 Hosting a Visiting Team

Mike McDonald

Whether you have decided to join a larger mission project or have received a call from a church that wants to bring a team to your area for a smaller project, you will need to think about how to host the incoming team. Hosting a mission tour team is a big task, but well worth the effort. There are challenges, but the time you expend is overshadowed by the life-changing experience your students and the visiting team members will have. Here are some thoughts on how to successfully host a visiting youth mission team.

Communicate well with the leaders of the visiting team: Get things in writing! It's not enough to try to remember what you talked about long after the discussion took place. Our church hosted the same team on two different occasions. The second time we were able to eliminate some problems we had the first time by discussing expectations and having written plans. From our past experience we were aware of different nuances in leadership style between ourselves and the leader of this group. This was a great help in working out expectations. As hosts, we communicated that the teens would have little or no free time, which had been a problem in the past. We also had all of our plans written down, using e-mail to send messages back and forth. By keeping track of these messages, it was quite easy to refer back to them and say, "Remember when we discussed this?" It kept everyone accountable and eliminated surprises. Leadership styles vary, and if one team leader is quite easy going and likes to change plans at the drop of a hat, it's good to have a written agreement to fall back on. This eliminates a lot of hard feelings on both sides. We don't need to be inflexible and have everything cast in stone, but there has to be a generally agreed upon plan or timetable.

Remember to make the plans as specific as possible. If one leader writes and requests something, the other leader can write back, reiterate the request, and provide clarifying details. For example: "Can your church host us for supper one night?" as an initial question, can be clarified when the other leader answers, "We can have our people put together a spaghetti dinner with salad, drinks, and ice cream in our fellowship hall. Can your teens each contribute $5 towards the food and help clean up?" This is the level of clarity you need. One group is still hosting, but the term "hosting" is defined as one group preparing the food, while the other is still paying for it and cleaning up. Every last possible item on the agenda must be thought through in these terms, to minimize confusion and potential problems.

Youth pastor Dale Stairs once hosted one of our groups at Kennebecasis Baptist Church in Quispamsis, near Saint John, New Brunswick. They did an incredible job hosting approximately 80 people from five different churches and held daily leaders meetings. Dale says, "It is very important to have both host and visiting leaders together for at least a few minutes each day to discuss any issues that may have come up, or things that could be done differently. The visiting leaders will often have great insights that, as a host, you will completely miss." He also notes that we need to "be ready for the unexpected! The visiting team will have lots of new ideas and suggestions. While some of these may not fit into the plan for the week, others may add a lot to the experience and ministry."

Have a well laid out agenda of events: If the schedule is written down and handed out to the students and leaders, you will reduce the risk of mutiny. A mutiny occurs when the teens and sometimes your other leaders, grab the schedule and study it with a view to skipping planned events in order to create free time. Most of them are looking for a few hours to visit a local mall, souvenir shop or amusement place. As tough as it sounds, don't allow them to create free time. Instead, make free time a scheduled event for everyone. If you make free time a scheduled event, it eliminates the grumbling. Also, don't put free time too early in the schedule but place it near the end of the trip so they can look forward to it and save their money. If you shop during the first couple of days, some teens will spend every cent they have and then try to borrow from others for the remainder of the week. This usually causes a lot of hard feelings.

Remind them of their purpose for visiting and assure them that you have their best interests in mind. If there is free time in the schedule, try to give enough structure so that teens don't wander too far away or initiate mischief. Conversely, don't make the schedule so tight and jam-packed that there is very little time to get from one activity to the next. There is nothing worse than feeling pressured to get from one location to the next, or having no time to unwind or debrief from the happenings of the day.

Know the exact number of team members: At a youth pastor's conference someone humorously asked if anyone ever knows the number of teens going on their trip the day before they are going to leave. I heard Rob Nylen respond, "Does anyone know when you are an hour down the road?" Although this was meant to be a funny comment, it illustrates that you cannot do anything about the last minute cancellation because of illness or family tragedy.

The situation is different when the team coming to visit you brings additional people. When you have a group coming to stay with you, it is important to know the number of people who are coming. There is nothing worse than having more visitors than hosts to accommodate them. If there is a last minute addition, what do you do with that person? Most times it is hard enough to find hosts for the numbers that you have, without last minute additions. Know the numbers, and make your visitors stick to that number, explaining that there is nothing you can do if they exceed that figure. Unexpected visitors will affect your billeting plans, your meal and transportation plans, positions available for volunteer ministry and your budget. Everything will have to be adjusted because of one person. If you think that your visitors might make a last minute addition, try to have extra hosts on hand. If there is a last minute cancellation, it might mean disappointing a host. Do the best you can, and trust the Lord for the rest.

Find out any special needs for each team member: It is helpful to know if any of your guests have special needs. One team took a young lady in a wheelchair on a mission tour. It was helpful for the hosts to know about this in advance in order to plan for things such as getting her on and off the bus, into various buildings and venues and even into the church building. One teen was allergic to stinging insects, such as bees, wasps, and hornets and had to carry an epi-pen that would reduce the complications associated with anaphylactic shock. He was not able to go on trips far from home, even though all of the youth leaders were trained in assisting him. I once worked with a teen that had Attention Deficit Disorder and required Ritalin and his mother told me that if her son did not get his medication at the right time, he was capable of putting his fist through a wall! Then there are teens that are allergic to dogs, cats and cigarette smoke and the ones that have special diets for whatever reason. One teen decided to become a vegetarian on the week that we were leaving for Texas! Have you ever tried to find veggie burgers or tofu in Houston? There are also teens that walk or talk in their sleep, who get homesick easily or have had difficult situations in their family life.

All of these things need to be discovered before team members are placed with an incompatible host. All of this information should be kept in a binder that remains with the group at all times. There should be permission slips for each teen along with medical release information. The binder might also contain extra copies of the schedule, curriculum you are using, copies of your insurance coverage and the lines for your puppet plays or dramas. Make sure all of your leaders know where it is and the type of information it contains. Of course everyone who is in leadership should know about any critical issues.

Budget the right amounts for you and your visitors: It's always easy to give extra money back. It's extremely difficult to ask for more money after an agreement has been made with your visitors. If you are budgeting amounts for meals or events, it is best to add a cushion to the amount that you calculate. Some people add a straight ten percent, while others don't incorporate the special prices or deals they know they will get. Be honest with your visitors about prices. When costs are less than what you first stated, that's a bonus. Don't forget to budget for contingencies. Make sure that you have allowed for parking, tolls, pay phone calls and even coffees for the leaders. A miscellaneous fund always creates room for the unexpected and helps to balance the budget when you are reporting on it later.

Be clear on the work and materials needed: Finances and planning are both affected by what is to be done and what is needed to do the job. If the visiting group is helping with a Vacation Bible School, they need to know if they are to supply the curriculum, craft supplies or any other materials. If they are doing a construction project, do they bring tools or do they need to supply the building materials as well? The work to be done needs to be clearly outlined. Are they just plugging into a program or starting one from scratch? Are they doing construction on their own or assisting another group?

Solicit others to help you with hospitality: Don't try to be the only individual acting as host. It is one thing to be in charge of the operation, and quite another to be doing everything by yourself. Having a committee to help find billet hosts can lessen a heavy load and dividing the work and making others responsible for different tasks creates ownership and accountability for the entire church. Are church boards and committees aware of what is going on? Have they given formal approval? Can you make use of the church social committee to help with meals? Is the director for the Vacation Bible School able to coordinate ministry tasks and find meaningful work for your visitors? The leader should be focused on communicating with the visitors and coordinating the overall program, but not doing everything on their own. Dale Stairs says, "I always try to staff to my weaknesses. If I know that I struggle with organization, then why not get a super-organized person to plan the more complicated portions of the week, like doing a food drive with 120 people so that no house is visited twice."

Finding host families: The task of finding hosts will require a thorough plan and some creativity. It involves approaching people and asking them to have strangers come into their homes. First of all, pray. Then establish a committee to assist you. Start by talking to the parents of your teens to see if they are able to host the visiting team members. The best-case billeting scenario is to have host teens and leaders paired up with visiting teens and leaders in order to unite the two groups. If you are still in need of hosts after this, then go through your church membership list and highlight the names of families you trust who have hosted visitors in the past and have had a positive experience. You might want to avoid putting an announcement in the church bulletin and making announcements from the pulpit. There are some individuals who will volunteer to host who might not be appropriate and then you find yourself in the awkward position of saying "no" to them.

Place visiting teens in pairs since most of them do not want to be in a strange place all by themselves. Also, for liability reasons, it is not appropriate to have a youth alone with adults. With the help of the visiting team leader, put two teens of the same gender that get along well together in a home. In some cases, I've had homes look after three, four and even five teens, but this is not recommended.

There is always a teen that volunteers to host a member of the opposite gender at their home. Let your students know that you are not even going to consider such a request. Tell them that it is a policy that you match teens up with members of the same gender so that their integrity cannot be questioned. It is not an issue of trust, rather of appearances. Sometimes the teens will attempt to have a late night party at the home of their host. This usually means they have too much time on their hands and that there are holes in the schedule. Try to have all of the billets lined up before the visiting team leaves home and send a list to them so that their parents have contact numbers to reach their children.

Communicating with your host families: Your billet hosts need to be aware of all the activities that are going on. Give them the group's activity schedule and a meal schedule so they know what meals they are responsible for providing and what meals the visitors will get at the church or at restaurants. The billets are responsible for providing a place to sleep, the assigned meals for the day and a place for the teens to get cleaned up or showered each day. The billets should know ahead of time the names, ages and gender of their guests, as well as any special needs they may have. If you are able to tell them anything about what their guests are like, it will facilitate both parties getting to know each other.

At the end of the first day, the host families should be contacted to make sure that everyone is settled in and the curfew time should be reiterated, after having been communicated up front. I usually tell teens to start getting ready for bed at 10:00 p.m., with lights out no later than 11:00 p.m. When the teens are dropped off at the church or ministry site the next day, it is helpful to wait around in the parking lot and talk to the hosts as they arrive. This way, you can see how things went and deal with any problems or issues. It also saves having to make a lot of phone calls.

Travel to the church and homes of the host families: It is best to tell the hosts to drop their guests off in the morning and tell them that the leaders will be responsible for getting them back to their hosts at night. Most folks are quite happy to do this. They feel they are doing their visiting guests a favour in the morning by providing a ride, but they don't have to wait around at the church in the evening for them to return. You can work out whatever arrangements are best for you, but make sure that they are consistent and well communicated.

Keep a sense of humour: There are so many things that can and will go wrong and the week is so hectic, that you have to be able to sit back and laugh at times, even if it means laughing at yourself. Then again, there are the requests from the teens that are always good for a laugh. If you can't laugh about a situation as it occurs, you might tell the other leaders "this will be something that we can laugh about in years to come."

Debrief your billet hosts and visitors: Debriefing can be done via one-on-one phone calls to hosts and visitors after the mission tour is done, or it can be done formally via a survey to them. If the visiting teens are being surveyed, do it the night before they leave or you will never get it done. Once they leave, it is almost impossible to obtain the feedback that you want.

By seeking feedback from your billet hosts right away, you hear about anything negative before it starts to make its way around to the rest of the congregation. Head off the bad news at the pass and share the good stories from the pulpit if you have permission to do so from the individuals involved. What you want to find out from your billet hosts is quite simple: Ask them if they would be willing to act as hosts again the next year, or at some other point in the future. If the answer is a quick and resounding "yes", that is usually all of the feedback you need. If you want to improve on your efforts, it is also a good idea to hear what could have been done better. It shows that you are willing to learn and makes you better at doing this the next time around. Sometimes the feedback might be hard to take, but later on you will realize that you have gained valuable insight and knowledge as a result. It's also good to debrief with your boards and pastors to see what they thought of the situation. They usually hear all of the comments, both positive and negative, and can be of immense value in helping to fine tune things for the next time you decide to act as a host.

Prayer support: Dale Stairs offers one last comment with regards to hosting a visiting team. He says to "remember to have a prayer team in place. You may wish to use an existing prayer ministry in your church, set up a voice-mail list, or have someone organize a group of people who aren't great with hands on ministry to meet for prayer while your ministry is going on." The importance of this should not be overlooked as our group experienced some life changing events as a result of the prayers of the people at Kennebecasis Baptist Church.

¶ Conclusion

Hosting a team is much more work for a church than being a visiting team. However, too many people view mission as something that is done away from home. Your youth need to be taught that mission is done both at home and away and thus you should consider hosting a mission team at least once every three years. By hosting visiting teams and sharing in mission locally, you communicate clearly to your youth and church that mission can and should be done on the home front. You will also notice a double benefit. Not only will your youth be strengthened, but also the ministry of your own church.

11 Being a Visiting Team

Mike McDonald

It is always more fun to be the visiting team on a mission tour due to the thrill of adventure and the opportunity to see new places. However, leading a visiting team is a lot more work for the team leader, and the benefits to your own church are not as obvious to your home congregation since they do not get to see, first hand, the ministry being done. There are a lot of things to consider when leading a visiting team. This chapter will raise a number of key issues, both big and small, to prepare you to take a youth mission team to the place that God has led you.

Make prayer your first priority: Make sure that God, not you, has chosen the place where you are taking a team. One church had made mission tour arrangements with a host church more than eighteen months before their date of departure. Eventually the leader realized that it had been quite some time since he had heard from their future host. The reason they had not heard anything, he discovered, was that the pastor who had promised to host the team had accepted a call to another church. His former church was willing to keep all of the commitments that he had made prior to his departure, but things began to unravel quickly, and eventually the host church backed out completely. The visiting team was now back to square one, with only a few months to go before departure. After much prayer, the pastor of the visiting team was ready to give up on the idea of mission tour in this particular area. As he began to make plans to go somewhere else, a phone call came in from the original host city and everything finally fell into place. Giving our plans over to the Lord makes such a difference, because only He can do what we are unable to accomplish on our own. Do not hesitate to turn over all of your concerns to God. If He wants a trip to happen, it will happen, but we need to bathe all of our efforts in prayer.

Survey the land: Just as the Israelites sent two spies to scout out Jericho in the second chapter of Joshua, it is a good idea for you to know something about the place you are planning to take your team. Take your camera or video camera, your best clothes and your best smile. Be determined to find out everything you possibly can. Make sure that you meet all of the staff at the host church and check out the entire facility. Attend as many of their regular activities as possible during your visit including worship, Sunday school, meetings, prayer groups, fellowship activities, or whatever seems important in getting to know the host church. Try the local restaurants and visit some of the shops. See what some of the neighbourhoods are like. Bring maps and pictures to show them what your hometown is like and how it is the same or different from theirs. If they understand more about you, it will help in building new relationships between team members. Take photos to bring home and ask for copies of the host church's bulletin. Ask for permission to videotape their morning or evening service. When introduced to members of the host congregation, make a point of remembering names and get a photocopy of their church directory. When you get home, circle every familiar face in the directory and try to memorize their names before you return with your team. Be determined to make a good impression when you return the second time with your teens and leaders. Your own group will take notice of how well you know everyone and can find your way around, which will instill confidence in your leadership.

If you take video footage, cover as much as possible, from ministry areas and conference sites to kitchen and bathroom areas. Bring home tourist pamphlets, restaurant menus, local maps, newspapers and anything else you can lay your hands on. While making your advanced trip, take in as much of the local culture as possible. Joshua's spies might not have been this thorough, but then they weren't dealing with the anxious parents of the teens in your youth group! If the mission field is too far away or too expensive for you to visit physically in advance, see if your hosts can send you some of the items mentioned above. If they cannot supply video footage or photos, find out what is available at your local library, video store, travel agency or on the internet.

Make plans with your host: It is best to write out a potential calendar of events for your time together with your host church. If you can do it together in person during your advanced trip, it will be much faster and easier than trying to do it later. Otherwise, discuss your ideas over the telephone and then agree as to how the calendar for the mission tour will be put together. It might be better for the visiting team to make initial proposals for the host to consider and approve or make changes. Phil Woodworth, the youth pastor at Cornerstone Baptist Church, Cornwall, Prince Edward Island, makes a point of having "a firm date as to when the details will be planned. For example, have check points leading up to departure for your team. At four months take a rough look at what the week will look like. At two months have all the details hammered out so that the teams can prepare all of the ministry details well in advance." After you have a completed calendar of events, make sure that the pastors and appropriate boards of both host and visiting groups have gone over the calendar and agreed with its various components. You should find that there will be very few changes during your time together and few surprises for either group. Clear and concise plans, in print, make a recipe for success. If you fail to plan, you plan to fail.

Present your findings and plans to your teens, parents and leaders: Again, Phil Woodworth notes "as your details become more focused, you begin to fill the parents in as the details emerge. Have a meeting at four months, then two months, and so on." When you come back home, show the video footage and photos to your teens, their parents and your youth leaders. You might show where you will be sleeping and eating, the church grounds and the ministry site. Show them all of your findings and outline the plans you have made with the leader of the host church. Point out what you see as potential problems and how you might deal with these problems, but be sure to add all of your positive insights about the wonderful opportunities at hand. For the parents of the teens, the highway might seem less scary and the sightseeing might look more educational. Regardless of your camera skills, the parents will be impressed with your research and will have more confidence as they entrust their children to your care. You will also be in an informed position to answer the questions of the church boards and the senior pastor. Everyone will be more at ease.

Travel details: No matter what the mode of travel, spend time getting the best deal. At the same time, Phil Woodworth reminds us that "in the effort to get the best deals, don't settle for poor quality. We don't want teens arriving tired, sore, or even worse, not at all." If you are flying, a travel agent can typically get you the best deal. Some airlines may offer, for example, one free ticket after fifteen seats are booked. In some cases, the travel agency might throw in a free seat to obtain the business of a large group. They will also negotiate the cost of travel insurance. Use the most commonly known air carriers and insurance companies to minimize potential problems in foreign territory. If you leave the country, it is best if these companies are recognized internationally. Tell your team that you are buying group coverage for everyone, regardless of their own individual health plans through their parents' employers. For the minimal extra cost, you eliminate a lot of potential problems later on by not having to deal with more than one company if you have an accident away from home. When travelling by boat or ferry, see if you can get a group rate or student rate. Most Canadian ferry operations are managed by the government and offer discounts to charitable groups based on the number in the group.

If you are using rental vehicles, check out their condition when you are booking the vehicles months in advance. One group borrowed the vans of a host church, not realizing how old and worn out the vehicles were. After numerous breakdowns on the highway, they had to rent new vehicles which they had not budgeted for initially. Regardless of the mode of transportation, find out if you have any students who suffer from motion sickness. Ask if they have ever flown or been on a boat before. Teens will put on a brave face before the trip, but the situation will change quickly. I've been seasick in the cabin of a ferryboat with ten seasick teenagers for company, as well as at the departure lounge of an airport when I discovered that nine out of sixteen teens in my group had never flown before. Young people have fewer life experiences, a fact we tend to overlook as adults.

Handbooks for each team member: It is helpful to create a handbook for team members and to send copies to your hosts before you arrive so that everyone is familiar with the travel guidelines of the group. It should contain expectations that you have for your students as well as devotionals for each day that you are away. You may also wish to include such things as maps of the host city as well as phone numbers for emergencies, the host church and key people. This handbook should also contain a schedule of the week, lists of do's and don'ts, lists of what to bring and what to leave at home. You may also wish to include the names of team members and personal data such as age, likes and dislikes, family members and interests so that the host church can know their visitors. These handbooks are useful to refer to before you depart, especially as parents are inquiring about what to pack. They also serve as a constant reminder of important details while you are away and serve as a set of rules that you can fall back on. A few blank pages are helpful for notes, phone numbers, and postal and e-mail addresses of your hosts.

¶ General Suggestions

Below are some helpful thoughts that you should present to your team to ensure that everyone has the best possible experience.

Travel Suggestions

- Please take quick showers.
- Make your bed each day and keep your sleeping area tidy.
- Dispose of your garbage in an environmentally friendly manner.

- Help with meals and clean up. Make sure that other people are well fed before you have a second helping.
- Be in bed at a reasonable hour. Any later than 10:00 – 11:00 p.m. and you will be exhausted the next day.
- Plan to leave a thank you note or small gift for your hosts.
- Have the cellular phone number of your youth leader on hand at all times.
- Stay with the group at all times.

Rules

- You must attend all events.
- You should be on time for all events.
- No smoking, drinking, or illegal drug use.
- No telling of jokes of an unacceptable nature.
- No gambling of any kind.
- No public displays of affection (P. D. A.).
- All long distance calls should be made collect, or on a calling card or call home card, not at the expense of the hosts. Do call home to let them know that you arrived safe and sound and that you are fine.
- If for any reason you are sent home early, it will be at the expense of your parents.
- If you can't say something nice, don't say anything at all.
- No playing of unacceptable music in any form.

Items to Bring

- The right attitude
- Duffel bags or suitcases or knapsacks – try to keep them small
- Plastic bags (to line bags/suitcases and for dirty laundry)
- The right amount and type of clothing for the number of days away:

  - T-shirts/tops, socks, underwear, blue jeans and/or shorts (1 or 2 pair of each)
  - Extra pair of shoes or sneakers
  - Sandals or flip-flops for the shower
  - Warm sweater or jacket
  - Nylon raincoat (optional)
  - Hat and/or sunglasses
  - Swimsuit and towel
  - Towel and face cloth
- Toiletries
  - Soap and shampoo
  - Shaving cream and razor
  - Toothbrush and toothpaste
  - Deodorant
  - Feminine hygiene products
  - Comb/brush
  - Lip balm
- Bible and pen
- Water bottle and sunglasses
- Identification – Canadian passport or 2 pieces of identification with photo and signature. A passport is generally required to leave the country, unless travelling to the United States, where a driver's license or school identification card with a photo and signature may suffice.
- Provincial health card and information on any other plans
- Telephone calling card or call home card
- Medication (inform the leaders)
  - Puffers
  - Allergy medicines
  - Gravol or decongestant
- Spending money

Optional

- Sleeping bag, small pillow and air mattress

- Camera/video camera
- Battery operated alarm clock
- Small flashlight
- Hair dryer
- Sunscreen and insect repellent
- Extra glasses, contact lenses and contact lens solution

Tell your team members not to count on doing laundry while they are away. It is very inconvenient to the hosts and it ties up a lot of valuable time in doing wash, buying soap, and finding coins for machines. Items such as hair dryers and insect repellent can be shared among team members and they should pair up among themselves to decide this before they pack for the trip. Raincoats, hats, sunglasses, water bottles, warm clothing or bathing suits are all subject to the climate where you are headed. Towels, face cloths, sleeping bags, air mattresses and pillows are necessary unless your hosts can supply these for you. Leaders should be fully versed on the details of any and all medications for the teens and for each other. If someone forgets their camera at home or does not want to carry one with them, they can ask other team members to have double prints made of their photos.

Items to Leave At Home

- Bad attitudes
- Ghetto blasters, Game Boys, Discmans, MP3 players or other such electronic devices
- Clothing with questionable sayings on it
- Short shirts, muscle shirts, short mini skirts, tank tops, two-piece swimsuits and thong bikinis.
- Excessive make-up or jewellery
- Aerosol or butane cans such as hair spray

There is nothing worse than having an aerosol can go off in a suitcase that might be subject to unusual conditions such as being walked on in the aisle of the van. Make-up should be discouraged or kept to a minimum. Although you may want to discourage electronic games and musical devices, encourage at least one person to bring a guitar.

Remember that what you might deem as appropriate may not seem that way to your hosts. On one mission trip, we knew the heat would be extreme so we allowed the females, both youth and leaders, to wear tank tops. When we arrived, we found that our host church frowned on that. They excused our ignorance, but it was not quite the impression that I had hoped to leave with them.

Gifts for hosts and small conference items: Always encourage team members to leave a thank you note for your hosts on the final day of your experience. A nice hardcover book of photographs of your home province, or some other unique item is always appreciated. Phil Woodworth suggests, "each team might contribute five or ten dollars and the youth pastor could purchase the same gift or card for each of the hosts. This way, none of the kids are feeling bad over a gift that is not as good as another teen's gift. This also gets rid of the have-and-have-not appearance." You might also want to provide items for your team members to trade, especially if they are going to an international conference or event. Small Canadian flag pins, provincial pins, or even buttons or pins from your home town are always nice little items and can usually be obtained for free from a tourist bureau or politician. One group had a lady make small brooches out of Nova Scotia tartan. Another group made a huge banner for their host church. It served as a lasting reminder and a testimony of the great work that God had accomplished during that mission tour.

¶ Conclusion

After the visiting team has returned home, be sure to send them a written thank you note or e-mail, which can be read to their congregation. This note might contain words of affirmation for the good work that was done to further God's kingdom, or it might contain a follow up as to what happened in the lives of some of your teens. Announcements could be made about faith commitments, upcoming baptisms, or future programs that resulted from their time at your church. Ask them for feedback and suggestions for such events in the future and plan a one-day reunion event with them, if travel distance permits. Tie up loose ends and keep all possibilities open.

12 Words of Advice

Mike McDonald

Giving advice on avoiding mistakes is like telling someone where to avoid the potholes in a road. It's one thing to know about them and another to catch them in time. These are some words of advice in order to help you avoid common mistakes. By considering these words, hopefully you can steer clear of the potholes.

Keep track of your teens: There is nothing worse than losing one of your group members and then worrying about them until you find them. Impress upon them before you leave home that you do not want to see their face on a milk carton as a missing person. Saying this may seem terribly blunt, but it will drive home the fact that you do not want them to be abducted, injured or never to be seen again. Many teens have no fear and may not even care about this issue so you may have to be even more blunt than this when attempting to get your message across.

Try to establish a small ratio of leaders to teens. One leader for every three to five teens has always worked the best for our groups. Most adults can successfully handle this number. Tell the teens that the leader they report to must know where they are at all times and be within seeing or shouting distance. Employ the buddy system, where teens are accountable to each other, along with their team leader. All team members, whether teens or adults, should travel in pairs or small groups, even in a shopping mall, to avoid any mishaps. One group did a lot of complaining to their pastor about having to do this, until an incident occurred in which they thought they had lost four team members in a very bad part of a large inner city. If the team leader wants to know if everyone is present, he or she only has to inquire of the rest of the youth leaders as to whether or not they each have all of their people present and accounted for.

Marlene Knowles, pastor of South End Baptist Church in Dartmouth, Nova Scotia, recounts a tale of her own regarding this issue. "In inner city Hamilton, one of my team decided that she would 'help' someone from the 'street' by taking him into a coffee shop and 'talking' with him. Her partner ran back to us to tell us where she was, but in so doing, was leaving her alone with him. She had a big heart, but it was a tense moment for me. So, being in a group of three always allows for a 'runner' if necessary. Four is even better."

Be aware of the news that goes home: Team members need to know the problems that can arise when news travels home. If there is an incident in which a member is lost for a short time, or injured, it should be the team leader that relays this information back to that person's family. The team that thought they lost four members all came back and phoned home to talk about the close call they had that day. The parent of one of the girls involved heard this news from another parent and was livid by the time she was able to speak to the pastor. At that point, the situation was well in hand and no one had been hurt. The gossip that went around at home gave this poor woman a terrible scare. Tell team members that no one is to call home with bad news, or anything questionable, until the team leaders have diffused the situation and dealt with all parties concerned.

Another way to deal with this is to have a contact person at home who fields phone calls and relays information, or gets parents to phone you to find out details on anything that happens. Again, Marlene Knowles continues by saying, "what gets 'announced' from the pulpit when you arrive home can sink or elevate your trip." Her situation in Hamilton turned into an awkward moment during a worship service when this teen readily told of her great moment in life when she 'helped this street person.' With regard to news going home, Marlene suggests no one call home at all unless it's an emergency. Once a day, the team leader could make a call to a contact person at home who could relay any and all information. With cell phones this will take extra effort to be controlled. The problem of news going home is not limited to phones either. E-mail can cause the same problem, but only worse, since it is difficult to communicate tone in an e-mail. On our last trip, one person sent a general e-mail to a connecting person who simply forwarded it to all families back home. This information was then posted on the church bulletin board and announced from the pulpit.

Let everyone know the lines of authority: Everyone on the team needs to know that the teens are responsible to the volunteer leaders who are in turn responsible to the team leader. The team leader is accountable to the church body back home and so the 'buck' stops with them. Be sure to explain to your team the results of their actions, both positive and negative, so that they can see the future implications. If the team leader has to field a lot of complaints from the congregation back home it could affect future mission tours.

Make sure that your volunteer leaders know that although you value their input, as team leader you are responsible for making all final decisions. If a volunteer leader wants to question your authority, make sure they know to do this away from the rest of the group. There is nothing worse than being severely questioned or chastised in front of your teens. Establish short "leaders only" meetings early each day where all questions, fears and anxieties can be safely aired. This would also be a time to lay out the plans for the day and deal with any questions at that time. If you are put in the position of being questioned in front of the teens after you have established that it should be done privately, you might need to reconsider the suitability of that particular volunteer leader on future trips. Conversely, if you are continually being questioned by more than one of your volunteers, you might need to rethink and adjust your style of leadership. You need to be aware of all group dynamics by being a good listener and taking advice from your youth leaders, rather than acting like a dictator.

Communicate your purpose and celebrate your accomplishments: If you want to avoid criticism about the value of the mission tour then you will need to clearly communicate the purpose of the project. Using the church bulletin, newsletter, pulpit and website, convey to the church what you are doing and why. Make sure that your senior pastor and church boards support the mission tour. Try to have the mission tour fall under the umbrella of a board or committee so that there is ownership and support. Remind the board of how much you need their prayer support. It is also valuable to have a commissioning service before you leave and a reflection service when you arrive home.

Our group always made a plaque to hang on the wall, containing a group photograph and a certificate, along with photos of any highlights of the trip. By listing the names of team members under the group photo, we established a permanent record of who was involved for future reference. This was not done to pat ourselves on the back, but rather to look back and celebrate the work that the Lord had accomplished through us. Just as the Israelites had a pillar of stones to mark what God had accomplished in their lives (Joshua 4:1–9), you should consider setting up some sort of memorial for your team and church members.

Anticipate vehicle damage: When you rent vans to take teens on a mission tour, make sure that you get all of the insurance coverage available, including glass and tire coverage. If you are not offered additional coverage, see if your credit card has this provision or if you can purchase it elsewhere. On one trip we had two windshields broken by road debris. The windshields were worth approximately $1400 each, but since we had purchased glass coverage we paid nothing. If there is damage to the body or interior of a rental van, the rental company can charge you up to the full amount of your insurance deductible, which is usually $500. With some rental companies, you can pay more per day for insurance to reduce the deductible down to $100.

Explain the cost of vehicle repairs to your teens and leaders. To avoid having to pay the deductible in one instance, the girls in our group used their cloth hair ties and bottled water to clean the grease off of the van seats. Avoid using a roof carrier for extra luggage as they tend to leak, dent roofs, and scratch paint. Also, the straps are in need of constant adjustment and you will always be concerned about low entryways. In one case, even after I had checked the vehicle height with the roof carrier, I still knocked one off of the rental van in a parking garage. If you think you have more luggage than space, consider using a cargo van or pick-up truck with a cap to carry your extra gear. You can also pre-pack your gear the night before you leave so as to cut down on unnecessary or excessive baggage. In the long run it will be worth it.

Buy comprehensive and well recognized travel insurance: You only have to pay one medical bill in the United States to fully appreciate having the right kind of travel insurance. One group thought they were getting a deal by saving a few dollars per person through a cheaper travel insurance company. Early in their trip, a team member broke out in a rash and had to go to a medical clinic. They spent almost three hours arguing about whether or not their travel insurance would be accepted, while it took less than twenty minutes to see the doctor. In the end, they had to pay up front for the visit and the prescription. Reimbursement came from the insurance company when they arrived home. The total cost was around $100, which was relatively small compared to what a bigger medical emergency would have cost. If they had bought insurance from a well-known company, they would have avoided paying the money out of their own pockets and waiting to be reimbursed. Many travel insurance packages also offer coverage for lost or damaged luggage and trip cancellation. With a large group of people, the chances are greater for a mishap with your luggage or an emergency or illness that requires someone to stay home or fly back early. These options can be added at little or no extra cost and are worth reducing your frustration.

Consider communication devices: In today's world of cellular phones and other such devices, make the technology work for you. Advise your youth leaders well in advance of your trip to find out how to use the roam feature on their cellular phones. Their phone provider can help them with this and alert them to the costs in using their phone in other areas. Using Canadian phones in the United States can be very expensive. Check to see if there is cellular service where you are travelling. On our first mission tour to Newfoundland, we found out after the fact that cellular phones would not work on the western half of the province, especially in Gros Morne National Park. In fact, at that time, there were no regular telephones either. The camp we stayed at used a phone with a satellite hook-up which was very expensive. The newer models of two-way radios are great for use between vehicles if you drive within a few kilometres of each other. They will also help to keep track of your group in an amusement park or mall. Make sure you keep extra batteries on hand. In the very near future, it may be cheap enough to consider using G.P.S. (Global Positioning System) technology to keep track of all of your group members.

Allow enough time and money: If you need to leave no later than 6:00 p.m. to make it to the airport or to catch a ferryboat, keep this information to yourself and tell your group to be at the church no later than 4:30 p.m. Tell them you need a half hour to pack the vehicles so you can be on the road by 5:00 p.m. You might not make it for 5:00 p.m., but will be on time for 6:00 p.m. If you get away earlier than 6:00 p.m., you have some breathing room. If you run into any problems, such as a flat tire, you have allowed your group a cushion of time to avoid missing your connection.

Try to pay for things as a group. If you give the group some spending guidelines and pay for everyone at the same time, you will always save money. Many group leaders give each teen their own money, in their own individual envelope, to pay for lunch. If you call well in advance, you can get group rates at restaurants and for admission to some events. Some fast food restaurants will let the bus driver or group leader eat for free if you inquire. You are bringing them business with your group, so they might provide some perks. When leaving an island, ask whether the gasoline is cheaper on the mainland. In some countries, you'll save money by having your film developed before you return home. Always pad your budget a bit to allow for the unexpected. Remember, saving time and money along the way allows flexibility to do other things.

Beware of the weather and other delays: It is so easy to neglect the daily weather forecast, especially since at times it is wrong. Nevertheless, you need to have a rain plan. What do you do if you were planning a picnic for lunch or going to spend the day at a water slide park? There are times when the alternative is not as exciting, but it's best to try to have one for any activity that is weather dependent. Even an extremely hot sunny day or unexpected freak snowfall can wreak havoc on your mission tour. Brainstorm back up plans with your volunteer leaders prior to your day of departure. On one trip, we had to phone the parents to advise them that we were sleeping overnight at the ferry terminal, due to an eight hour delay caused by a fisherman's blockade! The fisheries dispute between the fisherman and the federal government caused us to lose an entire day. Try to expect the unexpected. Use the delays as a real teaching time and also allow the youth to be creative in the 'Plan B' approach with you. You might even consider having a contest for a possible 'Plan C'.

Remember your family: Going on a mission tour may mean leaving some or all of your family members at home. As team leader, this might mean leaving your spouse and children for an extended period of time. Try to spend a few days with your family before you go away and be sure to build in some family time when you get home. Good advice is to have one day off after you arrive home, spend one day in the office to clean up a lot of little details after the trip and then take some vacation time. If your vacation time is going to be more than a week, arrange for someone else to follow-up with the members of your mission tour team.

Be sensitive to the fact that your family will not have shared in the excitement of the mission tour. Try not to talk too much about all of the great things that happened if they are not inquiring. Ask them all about what happened while you were away and realize that they grew accustomed to doing things a little differently while you were gone. It's great if you can afford to bring home little gifts or souvenirs and share your photos with them. Catch up on all of the news at church and in the community and remember that you have a lot of time ahead of you to share the stories of your trip.

Avoid the temptation of thinking that you have to bring your entire family with you on mission tour. This is especially important to consider if you have small children. If you are not going to open up the mission tour to younger children of other church members, why would you bring your own? Doing so will give you an extra set of worries that you would not have if you know that your family is being looked after, safe and sound, at home. Try to make it up somehow if you missed a birthday or anniversary while you were away.

¶ Conclusion

In closing, the biggest mistake of all is a lack of prayer. Pray with the entire mission tour team before you leave the church, when you arrive at your destination, during the entire experience and before you head for home. Pray without ceasing. Model it for your team and request it from your congregation while you are away. In turn, pray for your congregation at home. If nothing else, pray that the Lord will help you in avoiding these mistakes and other problems which might come your way. Pray for wisdom, direction, protection and team unity. Set up a prayer link with the folks back home. Ask your hosts to pray for you before you arrive and while you are there. Pray after you have returned home and praise the Lord for the good work He has done in and through your group.

13 Travelling with Teens

Bruce Fawcett

Everyone has his or her own "happy place" and things they do that bring them joy. For me, when I visit my grandmother's hometown of Bridgetown, Nova Scotia where I spent a lot of my summers as a kid, the air always seems a little fresher. There's also something about walking into my in-law's cottage that demands that my wristwatch come off my arm and the straw hat take its place on my head.

Travelling with students has also been a great experience for me. There's something about the excitement of the early morning on the day we leave. There's something about travelling down the highway to places some in our group have never visited. New sights. New sounds. New ministry. Summer without a mission trip is like a summer without ice cream – it's not quite complete!

For some though, travelling with teenagers has been a frustrating experience. Getting lost. Broken down vehicles. Unprepared teenagers. Disagreements among the trip leaders.

There are some things you can do to allow your group to have a better experience while you travel together. Hopefully some of the following suggestions will allow you to reduce your stress load and you can enjoy your students more!

¶ Why Travel?

Why would you travel with teenagers anyway? This chapter assumes that it is good to travel with teenagers in order to enhance your youth ministry for the following reasons:

To build group unity and identity: Much has been written about the importance of community in the local church. Without community very little ministry can take place. There is nothing quite like a trip to create community. If you want to see your collection of individuals become a group, a well-planned trip could be just what you are looking for! Shared experiences, and perhaps just as important, shared reflections on those shared experiences, are wonderful tools for creating a cohesive group of people and developing a sense of team.

Leaders build closer relationships with teens: Years ago, promoters of summer camp ministry used to say that you had more time with a child during one week at camp than you did in a whole year of Sunday School. The lesson here is that if you want to influence someone's life in a positive way it is useful to spend concentrated periods of time with them.

Travelling with teenagers for a weekend or a week allows leaders to develop close bonds with students that may have taken years by only connecting with them during a weekly meeting at the church.

To focus your program: It is very easy for church youth programs to slip into the "Friday Night Fellowship" model. The idea of offering fun events to keep teenagers away from school dances and off the street was very common across North America in the 1960s and 70s. The model was not all that successful and many churches missed an opportunity to teach their teens that the Christian life was not merely about having fun. It is about evangelism, discipleship, worship, service and mission.

At the church where I last served as youth pastor, we used trips to help us steer the entire youth ministry. If you read your Bible, memorized Scripture, and ministered in our church then we knew that you were ready to be a part of our mission team to go and minister elsewhere. Making a mission trip central to your program and not an "add on" allows you to focus on training and equipping for mission – certainly better for the individuals and the church than only playing ball hockey with teens for five years.

To attend faith-affirming and life-changing events: Many Christian teenagers sometimes forget that they are on the victory side. Jesus' team will win in the end! If the only other Christian teenagers that you see are in your group of 15 or 20 it is easy to forget that the church is over one billion strong. Attending large youth events is very important for Christian teenagers and leaders. The visible presence of hundreds or thousands of teenagers worshipping God, praying together and serving alongside each other can give some teens the shot in the arm they need to go back to their school where they may not feel at home or welcome.

¶ Assuring Parents

An easy thing for beginning youth leaders to forget is that when you plan a trip you are asking parents to entrust their most prized possession into your hands. The realization of this truth became clear to me that day I left my newborn son in the church nursery for the first time. No one would love and care for my child the way I would. Would he be alright? Did the people looking after him really know what to do if there was trouble? Twelve years later parents may be a little more used to letting go of their children than I was, but the fact still remains that you are asking parents to trust you with something very important – their children.

Here are some things you can do to build trust with the parents of your students:

Approve trip idea with church parents first: If the trip is more than an overnighter it is best to gain parents' approval before presenting the idea to their children. Is the length of time away alright? Is the cost acceptable? Is the time of year satisfactory with them? It is important to understand that non-believing parents may not fully comprehend the importance of mission and we should never be dissuaded by their lack of support.

Start with a small trip close to home: It is best not to plan your first trip with teenagers to another continent. Leaders need to gain the confidence of the parents by starting small and working up to a distant or cross-cultural experience. Some place within a one-day drive is perhaps reasonable to consider for a first trip. This helps parents to know that if something goes wrong they will be able to come and get their teenager.

Bring male and female leaders: On one of the first week-long trips I ever took with teenagers I went as the sole leader! The Lord protected me from the consequences of my own stupidity! What if I had become sick on the trip? What if the vehicle had broken down – who would have gone for help? Who would have stayed with the van? Girls have issues they can only talk over comfortably with women. Boys sometimes need to have man-to-man talks about issues important to them. Most parents feel more secure knowing that leaders from both genders are present on a trip.

Bring a parent as a leader: Often, especially on trips early in your ministry, parents will feel more secure if "one of them" is able to come along. This doesn't mean that they don't trust the 29-year old youth pastor. It simply means that at different stages of life you see different things as being important as you view them through a different lens. Parents tend to observe things that a young youth leader may miss.

Drive carefully at all times: If you are a driver who derives great joy from driving fast or laying rubber – purge this from your system. Parents want to know that you are a good driver. Squealing your tires and driving fast may win you approval from some of the teens in your group, but it won't with parents.

Mail directly to parents with clear details: Don't assume that information you give to a grade seven boy will end up in his mother's hands! Don't go with the cheap or easy route of giving information out at your weekly meeting. Mail directly to the parents. Tell them all about the details of the trip. The more confirmed specifics you can give them, the more confident they will be of your leadership.

❡ Keeping Healthy

When a teenager gets sick on a trip I don't know who has the worst experience – the teenager or the leader. It is pure torture to have a sick student on a trip. Everything must be reworked. Your plans will be altered and everyone in the group, to some degree, will "feel their pain." There are some things that you can do to keep the sickness to a minimum:

The longer the trip, the earlier to bed: A dependable maxim for a trip is that the more days in the trip the earlier the students should go to bed. If you only have your students away for one night then maybe staying up until 3:00 a.m. is not such a bad idea. But if you have them away for a week they had better be in bed before 11:00 p.m. If they stay up late too many nights then they will be grouchy and are likely to get sick.

Avoid multiple nights on a church floor: Sleeping in church basements is a wonderful way to save money and it is great for a one or two night trip, but it is not a good idea for a trip lasting longer than two nights. Some teenagers find if difficult to get to sleep in a room filled with friends. Most are far better off in a bedroom at someone's house that they share with only one friend.

Try to put only a few students in each room: If you have to stay in a church, remember the principle: divide and conquer. Keep as few students as possible in each room. The more you have in each room the more likely it is that they will keep each other awake. Remember, you will need two chaperones in each room if girls and guys are staying in the same building so bring along the necessary number of leaders.

Everyone eats at every meal time: I can remember being on a trip with high schoolers when I learned that the girls were not eating lunches at the restaurants we visited so that they could save their money to buy shoes. Now don't get me wrong, I'm all for coming home from a trip with a nice new pair of shoes, but not at the cost of your health on the trip! Students need to be told before they sign up for a trip that they will be expected to eat something at every mealtime unless their leader has given them permission to do otherwise. Even those who say that they are not hungry need nourishment if they are part of a travel experience. Students who eat are likely to stay much healthier.

Keep standard meal times: Not only is it important to eat, it is also important to eat at standard times. It may not seem like a big deal to you to have a late supper or lunch, but trips can be very demanding upon the body. Dependable meal times are very important for adolescents whose bodies are changing rapidly. Standard meals times can prevent grumbling and sickness and also provide appropriate rest and bathroom opportunities.

Dr. Mom: When you were a kid and got sick, who did you want by your side? Most of us would answer "Mom." Truthfully, many youth pastors are not quite as cuddly and sensitive as someone's mom. If you are not a mom, make sure that you take someone's mom along with you as the medicine person. If a student can't have his or her own mom if they are sick the next best thing is someone else's mom. Mothers generally have a good grasp of the basic medicines that should be brought on a trip and what they are used for, and are much better on the sensitivity front. If you have the luxury of bringing a nurse or doctor on the trip, all the better.

❡ Driving Tips

Bathroom/Beverage breaks = one minute per person: The whole issue of travel breaks with teenagers is bizarre when you stop and consider it. You stop at a gas station or convenience store so that they can use the washroom and then they promptly buy a large bottle of pop that virtually guarantees that you will have to repeat the scene in two hours! As bizarre as this "out and in" routine may appear, you nevertheless will need to stop about every two hours, and a rule of thumb is that unless you pull over at a very large truck stop, the break will take about one minute for every person you have with you.

The further the distance the more empty the van needs to be: If you are only travelling two hours feel free to fill up all the seats in your van. However, if you are travelling for ten hours in a day, people are going to need more legroom and elbow space. A van that is too full encourages crabbiness and fights and may result in a lower quality experience for all.

If the trip is longer than four hours, change drivers every two hours: There are some macho drivers who insist on doing all the driving even if you are travelling 1500 km in a day. I was one of them. One day I left Toronto, Ontario, for Moncton, New Brunswick as the sole driver for one of the vans in a three-van convoy. It began to rain heavily 30 minutes into the trip and traffic on Highway 401 slowed down to 65 km per hour. As I did the math in my head, I realized it was going to be a long day. Although the rain became less furious as we travelled further from Toronto, it rained all the way home except for a half an hour. The day that began at 5:30 a.m. didn't end until 3:30 a.m. I should have had other drivers with whom I could rotate.

I have discovered two things over time. One is that driving tires me out more than I think it does at the time, and if I rotate with other drivers then I arrive more refreshed. The second thing I have learned is that if you are driving a 15-passenger van it is difficult to fully participate in the conversation going on behind you. It is better to spend some time sitting in the back with the passengers to enjoy the community experience.

Groups should consider making driver rotation mandatory to protect some people from themselves and everyone from a tired out driver. Safety demands wisdom.

¶ Common Causes of Grumbling

Believe it or not, grumbling on a trip is predictable. There are certain things we can do to virtually guarantee that people will be unhappy:

Providing options during the trip: Trips are not a democracy. You should allow people to vote on activities *before* you go on a trip. Would your students rather see the Toronto Blue Jays play at home or go up the CN Tower? Let them vote and decide before, not during the trip. You can't squeeze everything into one trip so let them pick their favorite activity. However, voting on a trip can create friction. Allowing students to vote on a trip almost always means that someone will have to do something they did not want to do. In reality, if you had just gone ahead and done it they probably wouldn't even have known that there were options! Stick to your published schedule and don't open a can of worms that is best left closed.

Leaders try to tighten up rules: You can always loosen up but it is hard to tighten up. If you said bedtime was going to be 11:00 p.m. and you changed your mind to 11:30 p.m. you are a hero. However, if you changed it to 10:00 p.m. you are now an ogre. Be careful to start with rules that allow you to loosen up and grant the group favors.

Music guidelines not made clear in advance: Music can be a real source of friction on a trip with teenagers. Very few things are more important to teenagers than their music. To deal with this touchy situation you need to make sure that the rules are clear long before you leave home regarding what is acceptable to bring and play and what isn't. There is not really a consensus among youth leaders. As the apostle Paul said, "Let each one be fully convinced in his own mind." Personally, I don't like indiscriminant listening to the radio because there are some songs that are played which I don't endorse. I much prefer to supply music. My general rule of thumb is that if it is sold in a Christian bookstore then it is acceptable to play on a church trip. Males have a tendency to hog the stereo so it may be wise to allow girls and guys to alternate choices from their own collection or yours.

Trip leader too uptight: Sometimes leaders are "control freaks" and drive everyone else on the trip crazy. While you need to be responsible, we also need to be human and fun! If on a scale of one to ten, one means "I want to control every waking minute of your life" and ten means "go ahead and play in traffic, I don't care" – you probably need to position yourself around 3.5 or 4. Err on the side of being a little too careful, just enough so that when your students get home and report to their parents, the students report feeling a little restricted. This is the kind of feedback most parents want to hear. No parent wants to hear that their teenagers were never given a mandatory bedtime and that each night for a week they slept eight to a room.

Trip too busy or too much free time: On most trips you can do three things a day: one activity in the morning, one after lunch and one after supper. If your plan for a day off on a mission tour is to go swimming you may find that the students will get into trouble because they don't have enough to keep them busy. At the same time, if you plan five ministry projects in one day you may find that you are running from place to place and stressing people out because they can't get from Place A to Place B fast enough.

No showers: Most students can go for no more than one day without a shower and not feel gross, especially in the summer heat. Make sure that your accommodations are suitable. Most churches do not have showers, making homes or motels the way to go for a long stay.

❡ Common Sources of Anxiety for Leaders

Believe it or not, leaders often create their own problems when travelling. I've observed several things that leaders sometimes do which stress them out:

Schedule too busy: Leaders are often really excited about the trip they have planned and want to make the experience full and rich for their students. Sometimes this desire to have a great experience causes us to want to do too much with them. Sometimes we can't bear the thought of not doing everything we'd like to do.

One time I was taking a group of university students to the Boston area on a five-day trip. My favorite restaurant on Boston's North Shore is called Nick's Roast Beef. I desperately wanted to eat there myself and expose the students to the "Nick's Sensation." As the day progressed, I realized that we were just not going to have time to get there. As much as I was disappointed, I knew that to push it and go would be just one thing too many toward the end of a long day, so we ate somewhere closer to where we actually were. It was disappointing, but probably the best move.

When we try to fill the schedule too full we end up causing needless anxieties and we rush from place to place. The schedule ought to be full enough so that the students feel they are getting a rich experience but at the same time there needs to be some down time and a manageable pace to the trip.

Not allowing enough travel time: Youth leaders tend to be an optimistic bunch – you have to be in the business we're in. By nature then, we often overestimate how quickly we can get from place to place on a trip. When you plan your travel time from Point A to Point B, be sure to allow more time than you think you will need. What if you get a late start on the morning? What if you get stuck in traffic? What if there is road construction? It is better to arrive a little early then to always feel time pressured.

Not budgeting for all expenses: Have you ever planned a trip and then realized halfway through that you have not asked the students for enough money to cover your actual costs? Maybe the price of gas went up. Maybe meals cost more than you bargained. It is wise to have a miscellaneous line item in your budget that is about 10% of your total budget. If you don't need it – great, save it for your next trip. But if you do need it, better to dip into that fund than your own wallet.

Motion sickness, illness: There are few things that are worse than a student throwing up in a van on a long trip. You will absolutely have to get the interior shampooed, especially if it is a summer trip! Motion sickness, or illnesses of any kind, are difficult for any trip leader. Be prepared to roll with the punches. Comfort your sick student as best you can but realize that you will lose travel time and that they need to go in the quiet vehicle, if you have one.

Lack of clarity about who is in charge: As was mentioned earlier, a trip is not a democracy. There needs to be someone clearly in charge on a trip. Someone who seriously considers the opinions of other leaders who are helping plan and execute the trip, but is ultimately responsible for making the hard choices that will need to be made. I've watched serious disagreements break out between leaders when some thought the agreed upon schedule should be changed and others didn't. Make it clear in advance who is in charge and stick to it.

Forgetting directions: Every vehicle should have a set of maps assigned to it with the agreed upon route for the trip highlighted. You should neither depend on your memory nor in your ability to communicate clear instructions to other drivers to ensure that you arrive safe and sound. Take the time and map out the way. You'll be glad you did.

¶ How Not to Lose Kids

It was 10:30 p.m. in Bedford, Nova Scotia and the party was in full swing. We had just finished a week of mission with 400 teenagers in the Halifax region and we were celebrating with our host church all that God had done in and through us during the previous week. Then the phone rang. It was one of the mission event organizers. "Bruce, are you missing a couple of teens?" "No", I said, to which he replied, "Well, I have two 13 year-old girls who claim that they belong to you." My heart sank when he told me their names and I realized that I must have miscounted as we had loaded into three vans that night. By mistake I had left them in a church basement in downtown Halifax.

It is possible to lose teenagers on a trip. Perhaps nothing can frighten a youth leader quite like losing someone's children who are supposed to be in your care. Here are some suggestions regarding how not to lose students:

Everyone gets a detailed schedule: Each person in your travel group should be given a detailed schedule. This means that everyone will know where he or she is supposed to meet and at what time. If a student gets lost or separated from a group they will know where to go to meet up with you. Do not tell them and depend on them to remember where they are supposed to meet for lunch. In the midst of all the excitement associated with travelling in a wonderfully new place sometimes the details get easily forgotten.

Leader distributes cell phone number: All students should be given the group leaders' cell phone numbers. I have given students little notes that I asked them to store in their wallets in case they get separated from the group. On the note I wrote:

1) If you are lost don't panic. Thousands of people your age have walked around this city before.
2) Find a good restaurant, go inside and order a milk-shake or a pop.
3) Ask the waitress where you are.
4) Call my cell phone, tell me where you are, sit back with your drink and wait while I come to get you.

Middle school and high school students always travel with a leader: Generally no one under 18 should be allowed to wander around without an adult with them. As a parent, when I let my child go somewhere with another adult I assume an adult is always with my child, and most other parents assume the same thing. Even if high school students are allowed to shop by themselves at home, when you travel, most veteran leaders think that an adult should be with them or in the general vicinity. Legally, you could be in a great deal of trouble if an unsupervised student is injured while on a church-sponsored trip.

The need to stay with the group is made clear in advance: All travel rules need to be made clear to your group long before you leave home. With the possible exception of what music you are allowed to listen to on a church trip, the most likely issue that will cause students to complain is the requirement of staying with a group. Students need to be told that they cannot wander off or shop in a store by themselves. They need to stay with their small group at all times.

¶ Making a Trip Smoother

Experience is a wonderful teacher. Here are a few rules of thumb that veterans swear by:

Don't take a group anywhere you have not been: You should always scout out your destination before taking a group somewhere. Do you have your directions straight? Do you know what the place looks like where you are staying overnight? Are some roads temporarily closed? Are the restaurants you are hoping to eat at large enough to accommodate your group?

It is a good idea to arrange a visit several months in advance of the trip, after the preliminary arrangements have been agreed upon, to scout out the location. You should take a video camera with you and take pictures of everything it would be helpful for the students and parents back home to see. If you can get your host on video talking to your students and telling them how much he or she is looking forward to them coming, all the better. Sometimes even seeing some footage in advance reduces the tension a little for parents and your other leaders. It can also increase the excitement level for your teens if they can see some images of where they are headed.

Book rental vehicles months in advance and get the contract in writing: It was fours hours before our group was to leave for Hamilton, Ontario on our summer mission trip. The group had prepared for six months to go. The teens had been saving babysitting money since Christmas. Four months earlier I had booked a 15-passenger van from a local rental agency to add to our caravan. I had obtained the contract by fax and walked into the rental office with it to pick up the keys to the van. "I'm sorry, Mr. Fawcett, we have no van for you. They are all gone."

That day I learned an important lesson: the same way that airlines and motels overbook, assuming a certain degree of cancellations, so do some car rental agencies. I protested a little but the employees simply reiterated what they had said earlier.

Perhaps more due to the prospect of telling some of the students that they could not come rather than my own combative nature, I asked for the manager and told him that I was not leaving without a 15-passenger van. After he explained to me that he didn't have any vans available and I explained back that I didn't care because I had a contract in hand and I wasn't leaving without a van, he sprung into action. Eventually he rented one from another company and in turn rented it to me at the price we had agreed on.

I wish I could say that this incident was my only frustrating experience with a rental company, but it was not. Make sure you book rental vehicles far ahead and get the contact in writing. It is good to call the rental agency a few days in advance and confirm the reservation. It is also good to firm up your backbone before walking into the office as well.

¶ Concluding Observations

The cement floor gets harder every year: Each year of travelling with teenagers gets both easier and harder. It is easier because you are more experienced. You know the questions to ask. You know the issues that will arise. You know the solutions. In many ways, the more trips you do the more enjoyable they become because you can spend more time with the students instead of worrying about the details that come so much easier now.

On the other hand, the older the body, the harder it is to sleep on a cement floor and experience any kind of rest at all. Don't be afraid to do the things you need to do in order to still be able to travel with teens. If you rent a motel room for five people don't be afraid to say, "Guys, I've got to have the bed." Similarly, if you need a private room, bring along enough younger chaperones to make sure you can get your rest. There is no reason why you can't travel with teenagers after you turn 45 or 50. You just may need to travel in a different way.

Students do not necessarily have more energy than leaders: Often as youth leaders turn 35 and observe the vim and vigor of teenagers playing and running, we are reminded that we are not as young as we once were. Don't let the observations from the sidelines of the basketball court cause you to embrace the mistaken notion that you won't be able to keep up with them on a long trip. Teenagers are great "one night wonders." They can outlast me nearly every time if we are away on a trip for one night. However, travelling with teenagers often reminds me of the story of the tortoise and the hare. Teens can stay up far later than I can and almost function the next day on a weekend trip. However, teenage bodies are growing and changing rapidly and thus for a longer trip they need their sleep in order to function. In fact they need their rest far more than they understand and want to admit. Don't be afraid to assume that if it's day three of a six-day trip that if you are tired everyone else must be too.

Something will always go wrong: Taking teenagers on a trip is a little like getting married. You can plan far in advance, work hard at it and still find that at the last minute something will go wrong. Why is that? There are just so many variables and humans are fallible. As you plan and execute a trip always remember that something won't go the way you had planned it. Maybe your vehicle will need a new radiator. Maybe your host will be two billets short. Maybe someone in your group will get sick. Just smile and keep on going. Don't let the frustrations and disappointments prevent you from seeing the big picture, which is what God is doing in and through you and the students during your trip. Maybe God has even put a little glitch in your way to remind you that you can't do everything in your own power or that maybe He has an even better plan than you do!

Students often remember the "little things": One May weekend I took a group of students to Boston and we had a fantastic time. The weather was great and the Red Sox won. What more could you ask for? During the trip, I was pulled over by the police. It was late one night as I was driving down a country road on Boston's North Shore and I took a corner too wide, crossed the centre line and met a State Trooper while I did so. When we arrived back in the church parking lot at the end of the trip, what do you think the first teenager out of the van cried out to his parents? Was it, "The Red Sox won!"? Was it "Did we ever visit a great church?" No, it was, "Pastor Bruce got pulled over by the cops … was it ever cool!" Years later they were still telling the story.

Teenagers remember the little stories from a trip and these events are part of the community-creating experience. They are on the inside … they remember when. Remember the stories and laugh, even if the stories are about you, because before you know it they will have graduated from high school and moved away and you'd give anything to hear them tell the same embarrassing story one more time.

Have a parents meeting the night before the night before: Don't meet the night before you leave, because if parents have forgotten to purchase travel insurance for a trip to the United States it will be too late. Plus, each family will be scurrying around completing last minute details. It is better to have a meeting the night before the night before and collect the balance of funds and permission slips at that time. You don't need to be handling paperwork and money the morning you leave on a big trip. Make the departure as simple as possible.

Travelling with teens can be a great experience. With a little planning and forethought you can lead a trip that is more fun and less stress for you and all who come with you.

14 Out of Country Projects

Mike McDonald

Taking a mission team out of Canada involves many details beyond those that arise when travelling inside the country. These things are easy to overlook if you are only used to tackling projects in Canada. However, if you are aware of a few basic issues before and during your trip, things will run much more smoothly. While I was in Texas with a team in 1998, I met up with Phil Harbridge, youth pastor of First Baptist Church, Vancouver. Phil has been ministering to youth and young adults for over 24 years and his overseas experience is much more vast than my own. I value his experience and extra input which you will find throughout this chapter. Here are some tips to help you when you start planning to take a team beyond our borders.

Plan your time carefully: Do not let the travel agent schedule your flights with less than three hours between landing from one flight and boarding another. If the first plane you are on arrives late, you might end up missing the next flight and lose an entire day. With at least a three-hour layover you will have enough time to retrieve your luggage, clear customs, use the restroom and keep the group together. We learned the necessity of a long layover when our group had to spend a lot of time tracking down our puppet stage in the odd-sized luggage area and ended up in a line of three hundred people trying to clear customs.

Be sure to count on your first day after travelling as a day of rest with very little planned other than getting acquainted with your new surroundings. Let people sleep in if they need to, especially if the time difference is two hours or more. Eating and sleeping habits are easily disrupted and it will take a few days to adjust.

As group leader, you might consider being the first one up in the morning while being the last one into bed at night. This can be difficult if you are dealing with jet lag. Phil would suggest that while there is little doubt that the group leader should set an example, that does not mean they should lose sleep. If your team has capable leaders, then there is no reason for one person (group leader or other) to get short-changed on their sleep. Encourage your other leaders (adult and student) to set an example and help you make it a rewarding trip for everyone. If someone needs to be up a bit later or get up earlier, try to rotate it through your leaders or make other arrangements. Remember, sleep is a spiritual issue. There is no other way to look at it. If your team members, including the leader, are not getting enough quality rest, then they will not be attentive enough to hear, see and notice what Jesus is doing or trying to teach them. This is a simple but profound principle and often an overlooked detail. It is the simplest way for Satan to short-circuit God's desire for the team. If we are keeping our team too busy, asking them to sleep in impossible settings or trying to have late night fun and games, we could be working against the very goals that we have for the tour. Getting good rest is essential in the equation of spiritual growth. Don't take it for granted.

I must confess, as I get older, I'm finding that I need more and more rest, before, during and after mission tours. I've even made a point of getting more sleep since hearing Phil refer to it as a spiritual issue. As leaders, we should continually be evaluating the use of our time and how it reflects in our own walk with Jesus.

Keep information about your team organized and close at hand: Keep a binder handy with important travel information, phone numbers and addresses all neatly organized. You should have permission forms for each team member with names, addresses, ages, home phone numbers, health insurance numbers and parents' signatures. Customs officers may ask the group leader if they have permission forms to take young people out of the country because of the vast numbers of missing and abducted children in our society. In one case, a whole group was waived through customs when the customs officer saw all of the permission forms were on hand in an orderly fashion. When he questioned where the group was going and why, he was able to see the address list at the front of the binder along with a cover letter that had been sent to the parents of the teens.

Secure the proper travel documents: Find out where your group needs to go to get passports made, how much they will cost and the estimated processing time. This is usually done at an office in your provincial capital or you can mail the paperwork to the main Canada Customs and Revenue Agency office in Ottawa. Passport forms may be picked up at any Canada Post outlet. A few months before you leave, ask team members who already have passports to bring them in for you to see. Check the expiry dates and see if they are still valid for a few months after the date of your trip.

For younger teens in need of new passports, arrange a day to go to a local photography studio or have a photographer come to the church. Everyone will need to supply you with two photographs and their completed passport forms. The pastor has the legal authorization to sign the photos and forms of everyone known to them for at least two years. Take the forms, photos and total fees and deliver them or mail them to the passport office. In some instances you will require a visa to enter a country. The Canada Customs and Revenue Agency can advise you if you will require a visa to enter the country you are travelling to. Collect all of the passports and visas two days before you leave. Make two photocopies of the identification pages and keep one for yourself and give one to the parents of team members. This is important in case a passport is lost on your trip. If you present a photocopy of the original to a Canadian embassy you will speed up the process of receiving a reissued passport. Always keep the passports in a safe place when you arrive at your destination.

Again, Phil Harbridge offers a different approach more suitable for young adults. He states that because travel documents are now an arduous but essential requirement, "I have found that it is better to have each individual team member secure their own travel documents and passports." It is far too complex and labour intensive to have the group leader broker the groups' passports and it is also an opportunity for team members to demonstrate some initiative and responsibility for their well-being. Authorized passport outlets are knowledgeable of the details and can provide your group members with the needed photos. The only downside to this is that the team leader has to monitor and at times nag the team members to stay on top of the process in order to be sure they have enough time to receive their passports and documentation prior to departure. Again, this is a great opportunity for team members to learn to take some responsibility and leadership and it also frees up the leader not to have to hold peoples' hands.

Look out for health needs: Make sure that everyone has his or her provincial health card since a lot of their health information is encoded on the magnetic bar on the back of the card. Your travel agent can tell you what, if any, immunizations are required to travel to your destination, and you can arrange for your entire group to get their shots at the same time at a local medical clinic. Buy group insurance through your travel agent and make sure the carrier is recognized internationally.

Phil reminds us travel insurance is a must and should be secured with a primary carrier. Many travel agency health insurers are a secondary carrier, which means they will use up your primary extended health benefit plan lifetime amount prior to making any payment on your behalf. Primary carriers (i.e. Blue Cross, Great West Life or Sun Life) on the other hand, pay out health claims directly without touching your lifetime extended health coverage. If you are unsure, ask your provincial health coverage agent. It is always better to have more coverage than less, especially since it is relatively inexpensive.

Put one of your adult volunteers in charge of keeping track of health cards and medications as well as carrying the first aid kit. If one of the adults is a doctor, nurse, or has taken a St. John Ambulance or Red Cross course in first aid, they become the obvious choice for this duty. At least one person on the team should have training in first aid.

Tell team members who wear glasses to bring an extra pair along with them. One of our team members broke her glasses during a recreational activity with some children at the host church. Our group was due back home in a few days, so there was no sense in having another pair of glasses sent to her. For the remaining days of the trip she was at an extreme disadvantage.

It is best to advise the entire team to drink only bottled water, or water that you are absolutely sure is safe to drink. They should also steer clear of ice cubes. The same culprit in the water that will make you sick is lurking in the ice that you might add to your glass of bottled water. Check with your family doctor for any appropriate medications for your travel destination. Doctor-prescribed diarrhoea pills are well worth the cost.

Be systematic about your luggage: At one of your team meetings discuss different types of luggage and packing tips. Give your team this information early enough to allow them time to purchase any luggage items they might need for the trip. Soft-sided luggage packs easier and is less bulky to carry while luggage with wheels is easier to move. If items are packed inside plastic bags they will not get wet if they are set down in water or left out in the open when the plane is being loaded. Make sure you know the maximum weight your airline will allow each person to check and tell team members not to bring more than they can personally carry. Inquire with the airline as to the weight, dimensions and number of bags each person may carry on the plane with them. It's a good idea to forewarn team members that if they are over their weight limit on their luggage that they will be responsible for any incurred costs.

If you are carrying extra gear, such as a puppet stage, sound system, guitar, or craft supplies, put someone in charge of watching for this piece and have teens take turns carrying and loading it. Most carriers are fairly lenient about allowing extra for charitable groups. Use matching name tags for your group so that you can help each other find your luggage as it comes off the baggage carousel. Tell the team to put your home church address and phone number on the tags. If a bag is lost and retrieved, someone at the church will be able to contact you from home to inform you.

Be pro-active about your funds: If team members require foreign currency it may have to be ordered in advance from the bank. Usually only the main branch of a bank in a large city will handle large amounts of currency from other countries. Even if you are getting traveller's cheques in this currency, they will probably have to be ordered at least a week in advance. Inquire with your bank concerning foreign cash and traveller's cheques and watch the exchange rates. Sometimes you can see a trend with exchange rates and will be able to take advantage of a positive upswing. If the rate is higher than you think it will be by the time you leave, it might be best to buy early. With United States currency, you can open an account at your bank in American funds if this will help with exchange rates. In some countries, American money can be used as well as the local currency. As with travel insurance, make sure your brand of traveller's cheques are recognized internationally. If you plan to use a credit card or debit card, make sure your card will work in another country and be sure to find out what the transaction fee will be when you use your card.

If you pay sales tax in another country, you are eligible to be reimbursed. For example, when you fly back from the United Kingdom the airline will supply each person with a form to fill out showing their purchases and how much Value Added Tax (VAT) they paid. If you have your receipts handy, rather than packed with your luggage, you can fill out this form and leave it with the customs officers at the airport rather than sending for it later. Check ahead of time to find out what percentage of tax you will pay when you make foreign purchases.

Make sure that all of your team members are accustomed to the foreign currency and its various denominations of coins and bills. Show them some samples and how to count it properly. Provide a chart for them so that they will know the value in Canadian dollars. Be sure to instruct them as to how to carry it safely on their person. Divide the group funds between the youth leaders, so that if some of it gets lost or stolen, you have not lost it all. Try to determine before you leave how much spending money is required so that team members will have the right amount. Finally, try to have some loose change in both foreign currency and Canadian currency for dealing with such things as pay phones, parking meters and vending machines, particularly at the airport.

Phil raises a very interesting point when considering the use of your personal debit card outside of Canada. He says, "More and more countries are debit card friendly. This makes it much easier to obtain local currency without having to find a large bank. It also gives you peace of mind that the exchange rate is being properly secured through international banking institutions." He reminds us that group members should be aware however that debit card personal identification numbers (PIN) in some non-western countries should not contain the number "0", which is not recognized as a legitimate number. Your PIN can be easily changed at your bank prior to departure. By the way, don't forget about having some cash on hand to tip porters and drivers. This is not only proper etiquette, but could be a valuable witness to the generous character of our good God.

Check out the driving laws: It is easy to overlook the details of driving in another country since driving is something that we do each day without much thought. Find out from an automobile association or your travel agent if there is anything different you should know about the traffic laws and ask if there is a number you can call for their motor vehicle office. Driving requirements differ from province to province, state to state and country to country. For example, in Quebec you cannot make a right hand turn after stopping at a red light. In most Canadian cities in the winter, there are late-night parking bans to allow for snow removal. Some credit card companies offer car rental insurance that may not be valid out of the country.

If you are renting a 15-passenger van, find out the requirements for age of driver, class of license and type of insurance. In Nova Scotia you must be 25 years of age to drive more than 12 passengers in a van, whereas in Prince Edward Island the age is 21. In Atlantic Canada you are required to upgrade your license from a class 5 to a class 4 to drive a van with more than 12 passengers in it. One leader upgraded their license to be able to drive in Texas, only to find out that it was not necessary. The money spent to upgrade the license could have been saved if a phone call had been made first.

If you are travelling in the United Kingdom, driving on the other side of the road has two implications. First, it is a difficult adjustment for most drivers. Second, pedestrians need to be alert. You are, or should be, used to looking left and then right before crossing the street in Canada, but you have to do the reverse in Britain. I was almost hit by a bus in Glasgow, Scotland, when I forgot about this. You may need an international license to drive in the country of your destination. Your local department of motor vehicles should be able to give you some assistance. Tell your teens that they must drive in the vehicle that you or one of your leaders is driving and not with drivers from the host church. Their parents will feel more at ease, you can keep better track of your team members and if there is a mishap, they will have been with you rather than someone else.

Make an effort to learn the language: If you attend an international conference or event with your group, you will develop an appreciation for the importance of knowing another language. You will also see all of the difficulties in trying to accomplish even the simplest task if you don't know the language. Although your group will not be fluent in a particular language, the fact that you made some sort of effort does get noticed. If you develop a mission tour handbook you can include a page of simple translations. Knowing how to say "hello," "goodbye," "please," "thank you," and counting to ten is a good start. One group made a habit of watching the American version of the Sesame Street children's program so they would know how to count in Spanish. If you have to give any sort of message in another language in your host church, you must allow equal time for translation. A twenty-minute sermon in English could take more than forty minutes with the translation. Watch out for catchwords, colloquial expressions and cultural jokes. In some parts of Atlantic Canada, if someone were to ask if they could have more to eat, instead of saying "of course," they might be told, "fill your boots." When I said this in the southern United States, I was told it meant, "get ready for a fight." This made for a good laugh, but it could have led to a huge misunderstanding. Even in English, words can mean different things in different parts of the world. Try to learn some of these nuances in advance of your trip. Also, make sure that your teens know that jokes about any other culture, especially your host culture, are not acceptable and will not be tolerated.

Determine what is appropriate clothing: Be sure to find out what the weather will be like in the area you will be travelling to and if there could be any sudden changes you will need to know about. You might be in an extremely hot climate, but take a day trip high into some snow-capped mountains. Does your team need dress clothes for church on Sunday morning or are t-shirts and shorts acceptable? Will you get sunburned easily? Do they keep the buildings air conditioned to the point of being chilly at night? Are hats a necessity and should they come off during worship? Try not to pack too much and be sure to leave room in your luggage for anything extra you might want to buy and carry home.

Tank tops might be acceptable at home, but your host church might frown on it. Phil and I agree that "on our mission tours, we always ask the female adult leaders to handle any concerns or issues relating to the appropriateness of the female students' attire and the male adult leaders to deal with the male students." Phil notes that it's good to ask the local leaders that you are working with to give you guidance as to what is acceptable and what could offend in relation to clothing. We tend to think that it is the tank tops and spaghetti strap shirts that are the biggest problem, when in a particular culture it could be the board shorts and hats that the guys are wearing. The important thing is to not get caught off guard or to turn a blind eye. Deal with issues calmly, directly and with respect to your group and hosts.

Research the food and culture: It is a good idea for your team members to give you a list of the food and drinks they like and dislike. Then do some investigating into the types of food you will encounter. Tourist booklets and travel agents will be able to advise you on this. Check with your local library or ask around in your church or community to see if there are other people you know who have been in that country. Tell your team to do their best to sample the cuisine, but that if they really cannot eat what is offered to them to politely turn it down. You will find that most hosts will understand if they know your group is making an effort. An ounce of understanding goes a long way to bridging cultural gaps.

Your mission tour handbook can become a great tool for listing types of foods, different songs and a bit of the local history. It's a nice idea to know the cultural history of your host region so that you will be better equipped to understand the people. Tell your group that "when in Rome, do as the Romans do," as the apostle Paul modelled according to 1 Corinthians 9:22.

Know what you are permitted to bring home: Before you leave Canada, find out in advance what you are permitted to take with you and what you are allowed to bring home. For example, United States customs agents were asking if you had roast beef sandwiches with you during the mad cow crisis and were looking for uncooked poultry during the rise of avian (bird) flu. Coming home, they will be looking for certain items as well, often times pertaining to agricultural commodities. Even upon leaving Newfoundland, you must pass through an agricultural inspection station, set up by the province of Nova Scotia, looking for plants, soils or anything that might alter another ecosystem. If your van looks like it's covered in mud from a farm, don't be surprised if your vehicle gets hosed down with a chemical spray, or if they ask you to empty everything from the inside of the van. If your team members are planning to make purchases in the United States or abroad, make sure that they know in advance the Canadian dollar value equivalent of what they are permitted to bring home, relative to the number of days they have been away.

Post 9/11: Since the September 11th, 2001 tragedy in the United States, the fear and threat of terrorism has become very real. Since 9/11, I've noticed that Marine Atlantic now requires a complete list of names, addresses, phone numbers and ages of group members, prior to crossing from Nova Scotia to Newfoundland. The first year after 9/11, they requested this by fax, two weeks in advance. It is now acceptable to supply this list at the time of departure. Airports have tightened up on all of their security measures, asking a series of questions concerning you and your luggage prior to boarding. Things that I used to pack in my carry-on luggage, such as nail clippers, razorblades or a Swiss Army knife, must now be packed with the checked luggage that goes into the cargo hold. If you have travelled recently, you will most likely be aware of any extra security measures, otherwise, you could ask the airlines what sort of security measures you should expect.

¶ Conclusion

These very practical and helpful suggestions will ensure your group members experience all that God has in store for them. It will give your team opportunities to serve others and enable them to learn how to work together, appreciate each other's gifts and to communicate more effectively. Considering some of these suggestions will turn your out of country mission tour into a lifetime memory for your team.

15 Evaluation & Follow-up

Mike McDonald

Most mission tours are difficult to evaluate quickly because some results take a fair amount of time to quantify. They are also difficult to evaluate objectively because there are a lot of emotions tied into the event, especially on the last few days. To get an idea of how well the trip went, it is easiest to get evaluation forms filled out on the last day before everyone rejoins their families. The last hour of a flight home, right after a meal together on a ferry boat, or the last evening together before a long van drive home are good times to get feedback from the group. There are three ways in which this can be done:

Survey sheets: Before the trip, make up a simple survey with enough copies for everyone. You can ask open ended questions which require a sentence or two to answer, list different aspects of the trip and provide a least to best rating scale where participants can circle their response, or some combination of the two. General questions may ask what each member thought about the planning of the trip, what they learned, how they grew as individuals, or how valuable they thought the project was to the people they visited. These types of questions provide answers with longer explanations, but are difficult to tabulate or quantify. In my experience, teens have been pretty good at giving answers to open ended questions. Rating scale questions can be tabulated, but do not provide a reason for the answers. For example, you might ask on a scale of 1 to 5 (with 1 being "poor" and 5 being "excellent") how they felt about the travel arrangements. If they assigned this a 1, with no other explanation, you will never know what they felt went wrong. Any type of survey will only answer the questions that you ask. If you don't ask about a certain aspect, you will never know what others thought about it.

Mark Sypher, youth pastor at Brunswick Street Baptist Church in Fredericton, New Brunswick, states "it is impossible to evaluate the results of an event without establishing goals for the event. It might be a wise idea to involve the team in the creation of the survey to be used at the event's conclusion. Doing this will help team members embrace the vision of the mission before it begins, allow them to do personal evaluations throughout the week, and share more effectively at its conclusion. It is also important that when setting goals, the focus should be on giving versus getting." This is an excellent idea to consider and gives more ownership to the team members in the evaluation process.

Leaders lead small groups and take notes: You might want to break your team into small groups and assign a youth leader to each group. They can ask questions that you have given them in advance and facilitate discussion to get a response for each area to be evaluated. This gives everyone a chance to articulate their thoughts and feelings in an intimate setting and allows team members to share and bond with each other. This method is only as good as the person who is leading the discussion, as it may be coloured by their own personal agenda for evaluation. The benefit is that it provides good material for the same type of small group discussion with your leaders, at some point in the near future.

Group discussion: If you discuss things together as one group, as team leader you have the advantage of steering the discussion and making sure that everyone has an opportunity to share. One person should be designated to take notes, and it is important to attempt to help them to try to see the difference between their thoughts and feelings. This can be extremely difficult as most postmodern youth have their thoughts closely connected to their feelings. Emotions will be running pretty high, so it will be difficult to be objective. Undoubtedly, someone will say: "This is the greatest trip I have ever been on in my life." You need to get past their feelings and find out why the trip was so great. Your questions will determine the feedback you get and it will be difficult to avoid reminiscing about all of the great things that happened over your days together.

Again, Mark Sypher has another insight regarding group discussions: "In our group time, we like to sit in a circle and have each person share which part of the event affected them the most and which part of the event, they believe, affected others the most. We ask these two questions because we believe that every participant can answer these questions without being criticized since what they are being asked to share is based on personal opinion. We have team members speak in turn around the circle so that every person is guaranteed to have their uninterrupted time. The rule is that no one is allowed to interject while someone else is speaking. You may notice that we don't allow for a time of criticism. Although this seems contrary to the exercise, the focus of the sharing time must be positive. This will be their lasting memory of the event and we want students to remember the good that resulted from the missions experience when we ask them to get involved again next year. My philosophy is that the youth are quick to share the negative throughout the week as it happens. It is the responsibility of the leaders to keep track of these comments and record them at their follow-up meeting. As for the team evaluation, I say praise, praise, praise!"

¶ Follow Up

After you have provided some sort of outlet for feedback, you need to find some time to sit back and look at the big picture. Was the trip a success? Why was it a success? These things will need to be considered as you do the follow up work after the mission tour. Consider these things to follow up on:

Try to contact all of your team members immediately after the mission tour: Every time a group takes part in a successful mission tour, there are a lot of feelings to deal with after the trip. It is important to have a short group meeting before the trip home in order to discuss what will happen. Tell them that after people have come together as a team to do something of eternal significance, a lot of close bonds are established. Many participants will experience an emotional and spiritual high, regardless of how physically tired they might be. When they get home, physical exhaustion takes over and emotionally and spiritually they begin to make their way onto the down side of this roller coaster ride. They will no longer have the larger group at their immediate disposal, and they will feel very much alone. At this point, they need to feel free to call other team members, the team leader or pastor and reach out for help within the body of Christ.

As there are some people who will not reach out when they need the help, it is best for team leaders to do follow up visits, make some phone calls, or possibly attempt a group follow up. The latter would consist of three or four friends within the team that you are fairly certain will not mind sharing in front of one another. While this is a terrific goal to strive for, it might not be possible because of family vacation or other commitments right after the mission tour. If so, assign someone else to follow up on the team. Leaders who have been assigned to individual teens for more than a week should feel comfortable about visiting them at their homes or making a phone call to check on them. People are at their most vulnerable time right after a spiritual high and you do not want to see the good work of your trip undone by a moment of weakness in the life of a team member. I have personally found that on some of our best trips, every member had a good cry before the trip was over, because they were overwhelmed by the work of God in their lives. Tell your team to expect this and not to fear it when it happens.

Pay all of the remaining bills: It is extremely important to make sure that all bills are paid. If there were phone calls made while you were away and charged to the church telephone, you need to wait a couple of months to make sure that these bills are paid. Team leaders may have cellular phone calls that need to be paid for. There may be charges after the fact for something that happened to the rental van, or a teen may have had an item lost or broken that the group might want to help replace. It is not uncommon to have late rebates, discover group rates after the fact, or to have a refund for a teen that did not go at the last minute due to illness. In some cases you can apply for rebates on the Goods and Services Tax (GST) portion of your Harmonized Sales Tax (HST) which may take up to three months to receive. In another instance, we received a group rebate on health insurance and received a late refund. If there are no unusual circumstances, you might be able to clean things up within the week following the mission tour so that items to be addressed are still fresh in your mind. As soon as possible, finalize all bills and prepare a financial report. This report, showing sources of funds offset by expenditures, should be printed in the church annual report, and all receipts and records kept in a file. If you make yourself accountable to the congregation, they will be more apt to support such trips in the future.

Send thank you letters to everyone involved: If you were visiting a church, send a letter that can be read to the congregation by the senior pastor. If you were a host, write and tell the visiting team how you were blessed by their ministry among you. Don't forget van drivers, kitchen cooks, or someone who acted as a good Samaritan. On one trip, we needed a place inside to eat our lunch as the winds were excessive that day. We landed on the doorstep of a church in a little fishing village and had a wonderful time with the pastor there. He received a thank you note. If you receive a special deal from a travel agent or amusement park, they should receive a thank you note. This provides an ongoing witness to who we are as Christians and may open the door for future opportunities if you ever pass by that way again. Perhaps most importantly, be sure to thank your own team leaders for their sacrifice of time, and thank your congregation from the pulpit for their sacrificial giving.

Report to the congregation: The rest of the church body needs to know about what happened on the mission tour. You might be allowed a few minutes in the worship service, or you might be able to have the entire service focus on this. If your church has access to the necessary technology, try to set up a PowerPoint show so you can tell the story with pictures. After one of our trips, one of our leaders picked his best 128 photos, out of thousands of digital photos, and put them into a CD ROM slide show presentation with music. The presentation was 5 to 10 minutes long and we were able to make several copies of the photographs (not the music) for the teens at a cost of less than a dollar per CD. There may be a new song that you learned, a testimony from a team member whose life was changed, or a message from the people that you were with. Take the time and effort needed to do justice to the moment you are trying to recapture. If the congregation can feel some of your excitement, it will add future support and more participants to the next trip.

Have a team reunion: While it is almost impossible to reunite a large team after a successful mission tour, you need to try. There will likely be that one person who just could not make their way to the reunion because of something else on their calendar, but do the best you can. Set the date far enough after the trip that people will have the time and money to develop all of their photographs, but not so far away that the excitement has faded. If the trip was in July, have the reunion in late August or the first week of September before school starts. Bring snacks and refreshments, and provide a synopsis of their evaluations and a list of the bills paid and thank you letters sent. The group can help you with anything that might have been missed. Some people will talk about contacts they kept with friends they met during the mission tour and you might discover a story worth sharing with the congregation.

Submit your story to a wider audience: While your trip may not seem like big news to you, the local paper might consider it to be a great human interest story. A team of adults and students raising a large amount of money to go and serve another group of people makes for positive reporting. There may be a newsletter, magazine, or some other form of media within your denomination that would love such a story. Our puppet group ministry to small children received a few seconds of air time from a local news station in Ottawa, right after their lead story on the plight of children dying in Rwanda during the 1994 genocide. The station used the story of our ministry to offset an international story that left many in the newsroom in tears. Good news is not always easy to come by. In addition, tell your teens that when they are asked by their English teacher to write what they did on their summer vacation, they should not be shy about sharing their mission tour adventure. I have seen new members added to a team as a result of another teen's English class essay.

¶ Long term results

After you have completed your evaluation and looked at what went right and what could have been better, do not forget to pray for the people you have been with on a mission tour. You may see some teens and leaders go into short or long term missions or pastoral ministry, while others will seem to fall by the wayside. Encourage people where they need to be encouraged and let them know that you are interested in them beyond the trip that you took together. Helping them to see that you continue to value them is a parallel to the eternal value that God puts on their lives. After all, the long-term goal is that we are all together with Him, in His kingdom, because of our missionary efforts to lead everyone to eternity through Jesus. Pray for your team members, and leave the rest up to God.

¶ Note

Some of the ideas in this chapter were developed after reading David C. Forward, *The Essential Guide to the Short Term Mission Trip*, Moody Press, Chicago, 1998. (See Chapter 12, pp. 181–191, entitled, "After Your Return.")

16 From William Carey to Tidal Impact: Exploring the roots of youth mission tours

Bruce Fawcett

This chapter is designed to explore the roots of Canadian Baptist involvement in short-term mission and how it gave rise to the youth mission tour movement in Atlantic Canada. The chapter will propose that while the Atlantic Canadian youth mission tour movement is rooted in the historic Baptist commitment to mission, it is a fresh and vibrant expression of the contemporary Baptist commitment to mission.

William Carey: In the late eighteenth century the accepted view among British Baptists was that the Great Commission of Jesus to "Go … and make disciples of all nations" (Matthew 28:19) had been fulfilled by the apostles and no longer applied to the church (Thomas, 1995). In early 1792, William Carey, a poor, young, part-time Baptist pastor, wrote a booklet entitled *An Enquiry into the Obligations of Christians to Use Means for the Conversion of Heathens* (Carey, 1792) challenging this idea. Though well-reasoned, the pamphlet did not sell well and the author looked for another opportunity to promote his passion for world evangelization. Several months later Carey preached on Isaiah 54: 2–3 at the Baptist Ministers' Association in Nottingham and argued that English Baptists should embrace the Great Commission as a continuing mandate for action. Carey's words were persuasive and four months later the Baptist Missionary Society was formed to support Carey and his family who left on June 13, 1793 for service in India (Estep, 1994).

Carey and mission: Though initially inspired by the thoughts of "conversion of the heathen" (Carey, 1792), Carey's understanding of mission as being more than Great Commission evangelism (Erikson, 1983) slowly developed following his arrival on the shores of India. Carey, in his naiveté, had hoped that the masses of India would hear his preaching and instantly become Christian believers. What he discovered was indifference and hostility to his preaching. In Indian society the social and religious culture was so intertwined with the caste system that many people of high social status were afraid to become a Christian. Carey was forced to broaden his practice of mission beyond simple evangelistic preaching. He needed to gain the right to be heard by meeting the needs of the people among whom he was living (McBeath, 1987).

At first Carey turned his attention to linguistics. Motivated by his desire for nationals to have the Bible in their own language, Carey spent 30 years studying and writing about Bengali, Sanskrit, Marathi, and other languages. Carey also opened a school at Mudnabatty, becoming the first European to open an educational institution for children in India (Newman, 1901). Later, Carey and his colleagues opened a college, built for the instruction of both Christian and non-Christian youth in Eastern literature and European science.

Commenting on Carey, Bishop Stephen Neill (1964) writes, "Carey's work represents a turning point. It marks the entry of the English-speaking world on a large scale into the missionary enterprise – and it has been the English-speaking world which has provided four-fifths of the world's missionaries from Carey until now." While what Neill says is true, Carey's work as a Baptist pioneer missionary also laid a new foundation for mission work which still thrives today. Carey became an example of someone who exhibited a passionate commitment to the Great Commission but who grew over time to realize that mission also involved Great Commandment living as well. In Carey's mind linguistics and education were primarily meant to serve his evangelistic goals (Neill,

1964). Nevertheless, his model set the tone for English speaking Baptists, and others, that mission was to be both Great Commission and Great Commandment in approach (Kirkwood, 1985).

Carey and Canadian Baptists: Carey's influence would be felt beyond India and England, all the way to a land that would be known as Canada. His fame ignited an interest in mission that eventually resulted in the 1814 Baptist Association meeting in Chester, Nova Scotia voting to send its first money for missions to the Canadian auxiliary of the British and Foreign Bible Society. By 1829 the New Brunswick Baptists had made a gift of $70 to the English Foreign Missionary Society (Fitch, 1911) and by 1827 every edition of the *Baptist Missionary Magazine of Nova Scotia and New Brunswick* carried exploits of Carey and other English missionaries to Maritime Baptists (Wilson, 1980).

A conviction began to grow among Maritime Baptists that they should contribute more than money and prayer to the missionary enterprise, and in 1844 they sent out one of their own, Richard Burpee, as a missionary to Burma with half of his expenses being covered by the Baptists of New Brunswick and Nova Scotia (Torbet, 1950; Levy, 1946).

The impact of Carey's vision continued throughout the century and in 1892 Canadian Baptists celebrated the Carey Centennial with a special mission emphasis. This renewed emphasis contributed toward the growth in Canadian Baptist ownership of the mission enterprise and by 1911 Canadian Baptists supported 72 missionaries in India (Orchard, 1922).

Early Canadian Baptist understanding of mission: Highly influenced by Carey, Canadian Baptists maintained Carey's Great Commission passion and built upon his Great Commandment practices. Evangelistic preaching was clearly a priority expressed in what was termed "village evangelism." The missionaries would travel by ox-cart to a Telegu village, pitch their tent, and invite local inhabitants to "hear the Word of God." Services would continue from early morning until dark and the missionaries would frequently visit 25 or more villages on such tours. Frequently, the missionaries would enlist capable national believers to travel with them and train the nationals to undertake such evangelistic tasks (Renfree, 1988).

In addition to the soul, Canadian Baptists were quite interested in the health of the minds of the Telegu (McCormick, 1993). In 1875 John McLaurin opened a school on the porch of his Kakinda residence. The school generated great interest and had to move to rented facilities in town and his wife, Mary McLaurin, later opened a school for girls. It is reported that the school had over 80 girls enrolled within four years (McLaurin, 1924).

Canadian Baptist Overseas Mission Board: In early 1873, when the joint Telegu mission was being considered, the secretary of the Ontario and Quebec mission board suggested the union of all Canadian Baptists in overseas work, but the Maritimers balked at the idea of a common mission board. In 1887 the Maritimers proposed a merger of the two boards but this time the Upper Canadians decided not to participate (Renfree, 1988). It was not until the 1907 founding of the Baptist Union of Western Canada in the newly settled Canadian prairie that discussion again ensued regarding the structure of Canadian Baptist overseas missions. After much debate the regional mission boards merged and the "Canadian Baptist Foreign Mission Board" was incorporated in May 1911, with the term "Foreign" being replaced by "Overseas" in the 1970s.

Canadian Baptist Overseas Mission Board and Mission: This new board built upon the successes of the regional boards, increasing the number of missionaries sent out and the number of fields in which they served. By 1935 Canadian Baptists supported 98 missionaries (Carpenter, 1990), and by the late 1940s Canadian Baptists supported 136 missionaries in five fields of work (Torbet, 1950). Mission development in the 1970s and 1980s was driven by two innovative approaches to mission: Joint Pioneer Outreach (JPO) and Task Forces. Under the JPO plan Canadians would partner with nationals as equals and together enter an "unreached" area to engage in evangelism and plant churches (Allaby, 1986). Under the Task Force model, Canadians waited for a national partner to invite Canadian Baptist Overseas Mission Board (CBOMB) to send personnel for a limited period of time, normally 10 years, to perform a specific function. Frequently these assignments were education or development-related (McCormick, 1993). By the late 1980s Canadian Baptist missionaries were serving in 11 countries on four continents (Renfree, 1988).

A New development: By the last quarter of the twentieth century Canadian Baptists witnessed the rise of a new movement which claimed to be a modern expression of the historic Baptist commitment to mission. This new movement involved a new time commitment and organizational format. It also occurred in a new location, involved a new type of missionary, and was not planned or led by mission executives. Was it really mission?

New time commitment: In 1974 CBOMB commissioned its recently retired General Secretary, Orville Daniel, to write an historical retrospective. In the final section of *Moving with the Times,* Daniel (1973) identifies short-term mission as a key new development in the Canadian Baptist understanding of mission.

Daniel finds the root of Canadian Baptist interest in short-term missionary service in the Peace Corps, where a "pool of trained American men and women sent overseas by the United States Government to help foreign countries meet their urgent need for skilled manpower" (Daniel, 1973). In Canada, only three months after the American government launched the Peace Corps in 1963, short-term service overseas was discussed by the leaders of Canada's major universities. This discussion resulted in a decision to launch Canadian University Service Overseas (CUSO). CUSO was similar to the Peace Corps in that, according to the October 1970 CUSO *Bulletin,* it had as its goal to provide "young Canadians of various skills the chance to work in junior positions in developing countries requesting their services."

After watching the developments in the government and university communities, CBOMB approved the sending of short-term mission volunteers in principle and a medical doctor and his wife were sent to Zaire on a two-year appointment in 1966. This was the first recorded appointment of a Canadian Baptist missionary for a term of less than four years. By 1973, CBOMB had sent 36 people overseas on assignments of less than four years. Robert Berry, Associate Secretary of CBOMB in the 1970s, observed that the interest in short-term overseas service was spurred on in part by the almost daily portrayal of substandard living conditions in the developing world through the new medium of television. Some have also observed that short-term service was made possible through the twin cultural developments of the ability to travel almost anywhere in the globe in a 24 hour period and the ability to communicate instantly with almost anyone in the world through telephone.

New location: By the early 1980s significant discussion was occurring among the leadership of Canadian Baptists regarding the future development of the volunteer mission emphasis. Robert Berry, CBOMB General Secretary in 1980, proposed the founding of Canadian Baptist Volunteers (CBV), a joint initiative of CBOMB, the Baptist Federation of Canada and the four regional Conventions and Unions that supported these two ministries. Berry's vision for CBV, however, was that it would have a leadership role in short-term mission in Canada. The elimination of a distinction between overseas countries and Canada as locations for mission was in keeping with recent developments in missiological thought among other North American evangelicals. The distinction between "home" and "overseas" was beginning to crumble.

Berry's proposal, including the notion of Canada as a new location for nationally-initiated mission and the removal of a minimum age restriction for missionaries was approved by the CBOMB board on October 5, 1987. CBV eventually secured approval and funding and in late 1987 Heather Steeves, a former seminary-trained CBOMB missionary nurse, was appointed as the first CBV National Coordinator, based in the Toronto headquarters of CBOMB (Steeves, 1998).

New form: The permission for CBV to operate in Canada and the removal of the minimum age restriction for mission involvement opened the door for a new development in Canadian Baptist mission – the youth mission tour.

The first of these summer events, instigated and nurtured by CBV's Heather Steeves, but organized by local groups of pastors and youth pastors, took place in 1989 in south western New Brunswick and attracted 69 youth and leaders (Steeves, 1998).

While somewhat similar mission tour events such as Team Up '96, attracting 145 youth and leaders (Drysdale, 1996), took place in Hamilton, Ontario, and Go Coastal '98, attracting 75 youth and leaders, took place in Vancouver, British Columbia (Steeves, 1998), it was the Maritimers who would most heartily embrace and develop the mission tour concept.

Mission tours were one-week summer events when local churches in a chosen geographic target area invited visiting churches to partner with them in a week of mission. A local church provided billet accommodations and meals to their partner church in exchange for sharing in the leadership of its ministry events.

In the mornings, the partners led evangelistically-focused programs for children such as Vacation Bible Schools, Backyard Bible Clubs, or evangelistic outreaches in a park, community center, or low-income housing project. On one afternoon one-third of the groups joined together for a Concert of Prayer to provide prayer support for the other groups who were involved in ministry projects during that afternoon. The groups rotated during the week and on two of the other afternoons the groups took part in evangelistic or social action ministry electives. These activities included food drives, serving at a food bank, or sorting used clothing at a clothing bank. Some of the other afternoon activities included an organized fun event or an afternoon off.

In the evenings there was usually a rally for all the teams participating in the mission tour. The rallies included contemporary worship and preaching. On one evening there was a fun event. In the course of the week there was also time set aside for the host and visiting churches to build friendships and relax.

The extent to which the youth mission tour differed from anything likely conceived of by Orville Daniel is illustrated by the development of the public rally concept which reached its apex at

Tidal Impact 2002 in Moncton, New Brunswick. The public rallies were designed to allow an opportunity for the youth to showcase their ministry involvement of the previous week to their parents, billet hosts, and other interested members of the host community. Organizers rented the Moncton Coliseum to accommodate the youth and their guests. The rally attracted over 3200 attendees on a summer Friday night (Trail, 2002) and apparently made an impression on attendees. *Tidings*, the missionary magazine of Atlantic Baptist Women, reported that one person attending the rally was so overwhelmed by the sight of the parade of 1100 youth and leaders marching into the Coliseum that she "just sat down and cried" (Stairs, 2002).

New missionaries: Orville Daniel wrote excitedly in 1973 about the doors of service that he anticipated would open up for "young people" but his examples of "doctors" and "nurses" and "couples" suggested that his understanding of young people were people in their twenties and thirties (Daniel, 1973). By 2002, however, the bulk of the missionaries involved with CBV were, in fact, teenagers serving on youth mission tours. In 1995 approximately 450 youth and leaders were registered for Bold and Alive '95 whereas the total number of reported Canadian Baptist Volunteers that year was 557. By 2002 approximately 1100 teenagers and leaders registered for Tidal Impact whereas the total number of reported Canadian Baptist Volunteers that year was 1239.

In only 12 years the attendance at the summer youth mission tours grew from 69 to over 1100 teenagers and leaders (Stairs, 2002). The 1100 youth and leaders who attended Tidal Impact 2002 represented a number roughly equivalent to one-third of the total weekly youth group attendance in Atlantic Baptist churches (Gardner, 2001).

Maritime Baptists had seen large groups of young people attend denominational events before. The annual May weekend youth conference known as Springforth, for instance, was attracting over 1900 students and leaders by 2003 (Gardner, 2003). However, the mission tours were unique in terms of the demands they placed on the participants. The teenagers not only had to give up a week's work to attend the summer event, they also had to pay their own costs, which were roughly equivalent to a week's earnings from an adolescent's summer job. In addition, the youth were expected to train for several months for the ministry tasks they were to undertake.

The mission tours demanded a significant commitment and a new generation of young missionaries rose to the demands placed upon them in increasing numbers.

New leadership: Crucial to the growth and development of the youth mission tour movement was the simultaneous phenomenon of increasing numbers of churches appointing youth pastors. Historically, youth ministries in Canadian Baptist churches were led by the local church pastor with significant support from laypeople.

However, by the 1980s and 1990s, mirroring a wider trend, and motivated by a struggle to hold on to their youth, churches increasingly turned to paid staff to provide leadership to their youth ministries. The loss of allegiance among older adolescents is illustrated in a 1999 youth ministry survey of Atlantic Baptist churches. This survey demonstrated that for every two 12–14 year old students attending youth groups, there was only one 15–18 year old student (Fawcett, 2000). Although formerly identified by the United Nations as a predominantly Christian country, Canada was reclassified in 1998 as a secular society (Johnstone and Mandryk, 2001). In response to the attraction of the new secular society, local churches were increasingly turning to professional youth ministry "experts" to lead their outreach to adolescents. In this context, both Atlantic Baptist University and Acadia Divinity College designed and implemented training programs for youth ministry staff (McDonald, 2001; Crowell, 2001). In 1984, only 21 ministers functioned as junior staff members in a local church, primarily overseeing ministries to teenagers (Thompson, 1984). By 1999, at least 74 churches employed youth pastors (Fawcett, 2000).

The churches, however, were not merely motivated by fear of loss. Popular North American youth ministry authors like Fields (1998), Borgman (1997), and Burns (1988) encouraged churches to structure and carry out their youth ministries to capitalize on the opportunity for rapid spiritual growth in the adolescent years. Typical job descriptions for Baptist youth pastors in Atlantic Canada centred on the mandate to assist young people in their spiritual growth.

Given this mandate and the full-time hours available for planning and leading events, many youth pastors found that their role developed, in part, into that of mission strategist and mission team leader. For many churches, the youth mission tour became a highlight of the youth ministry program. It was a big event that the youth anticipated by raising funds and participating in training programs. Youth pastors became the primary leaders of local church youth mission teams.

A new wind was blowing in the field of mission leadership. Newly hired youth pastors were providing the organizational muscle that caused the mission tour movement to grow.

Same intent: Carey practiced a form of mission that contained Great Commission and Great Commandment activity. Atlantic Baptist youth mission strategists planned mission events with a similar intent. A quick glance at early writings may not clearly reveal this link between the mission tours and historic Baptist priorities. The organizers of Bold and Alive '95 published a mission statement for the event that stated their mandate "To equip teens to be bold and courageous disciples of Jesus Christ through the practical application of their faith." Even their theme verses, Joshua 1:6–8, spoke of the aim of assisting young Christians to become courageous followers of God. Similarly, organizers of Tidal Impact 2002 stated their aim for their event as "to assist Christian teens in becoming mature disciples of Jesus Christ through the practical application and celebration of their faith" (Fawcett and McDonald, 2001).

However, a second look reveals that mission involvement and not just personal impact was a clear goal of the movement. In *Effective Evangelism in Atlantic Canada* (Fawcett, et. al., 2001), Tidal Impact 2002 organizers wrote: "In addition to training for leadership and involvement for social action, mission tours are also about giving teens front line experience in evangelism." Likewise, in a book written primarily as a preparation manual for Tidal Impact 2002 leaders, entitled *Youth Mission Tours*, author Michael McDonald, in describing the rationale for taking a group of youth on a mission tour, writes of evangelism and social action: "they are two wings of the same bird. You cannot have one without the other. One does not lead to the other or become a means to display the other; rather, one cannot exist without the other. People have material needs to which we should minister, and this ministry should be accompanied by the message of God's love" (Fawcett and McDonald, 2001). Even the motto for Tidal Impact 2000 and 2002 events, "Love God. Love Others", demonstrates that while the inner growth of the participants was viewed as a key element, the commitment to look beyond oneself in service to others remained.

¶ Conclusion

The youth mission tour movement in Atlantic Canada was clearly different from mission initiatives previously undertaken by Canadian Baptists. A one-week project was short, even by the standards of a group who had embraced "short-term" mission several decades earlier. The focus on ministry "at home", rather than overseas, was part of a new national understanding of the location for Canadian Baptist mission. The form of the event with worship rallies and fun events was unlike any mission event seen to date. The movement involved a younger age of missionaries than Canadian Baptist churches were accustomed to commissioning. Mission strategies and events that were planned and executed by youth pastors rather than mission board staff were also new for Canadian Baptists.

However, the movement, as demonstrated above, can, and should, be clearly understood as a contemporary expression of the historic Canadian Baptist understanding of mission. While the organizers exhibited a concern for the spiritual growth and development of their youth, the same passion for Great Commission and Great Commandment mission that was seen in the ministry of William Carey was still present among Canadian Baptists three centuries later.

¶ Bibliography

Allaby, E. (1986). Entrance to a gallery. *The Enterprise*. Fall 1986.

Borgman, D. (1997). *When Kumbaya is Not Enough*. Peabody, MA, Hendrickson.

Burns, J. (1988). *The Youth Builder*. Eugene, OR, Harvest House.

Carey, W. (1792). *An Enquiry into the Obligations of Christians to Use Means for the Conversion of the Heathen*. Leicester, Ann Ireland.

Carpenter, J. and Shenk, W. (eds.) (1990). *Earthen Vessels: American Evangelicals and foreign missions 1880–1980*. Grand Rapids, MI, Eerdmans.

Crowell, S., (ed.) (2001). *Atlantic Baptist University Calendar 2000–01*. Atlantic Baptist University.

CUSO (1970). CUSO *Bulletin*, Toronto, Canadian Universities Service Overseas.

Daniel, O. (1973). *Moving With the Times*. Toronto, Canadian Baptist Overseas Mission Board

Drysdale, V. (1996). Team up. *Canadian Baptist*. September 1996, 22–24

Erickson, M.J. (1983). *Christian Theology*. Grand Rapids, MI, Baker.

Estep, W. (1994). *Whole Gospel Whole World*. Nashville, TE, Broadman and Holman.

Fawcett, B. (2000). Effective youth ministry in Atlantic Canada. *Atlantic Baptist*. Summer 2000, 12–17.

Fawcett, B. and McDonald, M. (2001). *Youth Mission Tours*. Saint John, NB, United Baptist Convention of the Atlantic Provinces.

Fawcett, B., McMullin, S., Morehouse, D. and Vincent, K, (eds.) (2001). *Effective Evangelism in Atlantic Canada*. Saint John, NB, United Baptist Convention of the Atlantic Provinces.

Fields, D. (1998). *Purpose Driven Youth Ministry*. Grand Rapids, MI, Zondervan.

Fitch, E. (1911). *The Baptists of Canada*. Standard.

Gardner, H. (ed.) *2001 Yearbook of the Convention of Atlantic Baptist Churches*. Saint John, NB, Convention of Atlantic Baptist Churches.

Gardner, H. (ed.) *2002 Yearbook of the Convention of Atlantic Baptist Churches*. Saint John, NB, Convention of Atlantic Baptist Churches.

Johnstone, P. and Mandryk, J. (2001). *Operation World*. London, Paternoster.

Kane, J.H. (1981). *The Christian World Mission: today and tomorrow*. Grand Rapids, MI, Baker.

Kirkwood, D. (1985). *Between Heritage and Hope*. Valley Forge, PA, International Ministries ABC/USA.

Levy, G. (1946). *The Baptists of the Maritime Provinces*. Saint John, NB, Barnes-Hopkins.

Lum, A. (1982). *A Hitchhikers Guide to Missions*. Downers Grove, IL, Inter-Varsity.
McBeath, L. (1987). *The Baptist Heritage*. Nashville, TN, Broadman.
McDonald, L. (ed.). *Acadia Divinity College 2001–2002 Calendar*. Acadia Divinity College.
McLaurin, M. (1924). On the Field of Battle in Orchard, M. and K. McLaurin, *The Enterprise*. Toronto, ON, Canadian Baptist Overseas Mission Board.
Neill, S. (1964). *A History of Christian Mission*. Baltimore, MD, Penguin.
Newman, A. (1901). *A History of Baptist Achievement*. Philadelphia, PA, American Baptist Publication Society.
Orchard, M. (1922). *Canadian Baptists at Work in India*. Toronto, ON, Canadian Baptist Foreign Mission Board.
Orchard, M. and K. McLaurin. (1924) *The Enterprise*. Canadian Baptist Foreign Mission Board.
Renfree, H. (1988). *Heritage and Horizon: the Baptist story in Canada*. Toronto, ON, Canadian Baptist Federation.
Stairs, D. Tidal Impact 2002: One mission: Two cities. *Tidings*. December, 2002, 12.
Steeves, H. (1998). Mixing up your summer. *A Season for Service*. Fall, 1998, 1–5.
Thomas, N (ed.) (1995). *Classic Texts in Mission and World Christianity*. Maryknoll, NY, Orbis.
Thompson, E. (1984). *Yearbook of the United Baptist Convention of the Atlantic Provinces*. Saint John, NB, United Baptist Convention of the Atlantic Provinces.
Torbet, R. (1950). *A History of the Baptists*. Philadelphia, PA, Judson.
Torbet, R. (1955). *Venture of Faith*. Philadelphia, PA, Judson.
Trail, D. (2002). Mega-missions event floods Maritimes. *Christian Week*. September 17, 2002.
Wilson, R. (1980). British influence in the nineteen century. in Zeman, J. (ed.) *Baptists in Canada*. Burlington ON, Welch.
Zeman, J. (1978). *Baptist Roots and Identity*. Toronto ON, Baptist Convention of Ontario and Quebec.

17 Large Mission Tours in Atlantic Canada

Bruce Fawcett

By the late 1980s there were youth ministries in perhaps a dozen Baptist churches across the Atlantic Provinces that were regularly sending out youth mission teams each summer. Many of these churches were following the example of First Baptist Church in Dartmouth, Nova Scotia, and its pastor, David Watt. By 1989 a new development in the mission tour movement took place when several groups began to plan their own church's mission tours to coincide with the tours of other churches so that their teenagers could work side by side. This cooperation brought a new power and energy to this movement and resulted in significant growth in the lives of teenagers from across Atlantic Canada and beyond. What follows is a brief description of the growth and development of the major youth mission tour events in Eastern Canada.

Southwestern New Brunswick 1989: In the summer of 1989 five youth teams joined together in a week of mission. The groups cooperated in hosting morning outreaches to children, public witness in parks and evening gatherings for study and worship. In addition, the groups enjoyed several fun events together. The event was not large, involving 69 people, but it did mark a significant new step in the approach to youth mission in this region of Canada.

This youth mission project demonstrated that cooperation in mission, which was a key force in bringing together two Baptist groups that formed the United Baptist Convention in 1905/06, was still a powerful unifying force. Some of the teenagers who served alongside each other formed lifelong friendships and many attested to a strong work of God in their lives during the week long project.

The experience was also very positive for the leaders, providing fellowship and encouragement for the youth pastors who served on ministry's front lines. (For a list of organizers of this project and others see Appendix 6.)

Urban Impact 1992: A joint Wesleyan/Baptist urban ministries camp called Urban Impact was held in the Saint John region in the summer of 1992. Urban Impact derived some of its inspiration from the spirit of mission encouraged during the Canadian Baptist Federation youth conference the previous summer. A dozen groups were involved in mission before and after the Charlottetown, Prince Edward Island conference.

Attended by approximately 150 teenagers, the Urban Impact residential camp was based at Rothesay Baptist Church. It was designed to provide training for urban ministry each morning. This training was followed up by practical application of the newly acquired ministry skills in the streets of Saint John in the afternoon. The event also featured evening rallies at Saint John High School with featured worship leader Will McFarlane of Nashville, Tennessee and local speaker Larry Mitchell.

While the "camp" model was not repeated due to the high cost associated with catered meals and the challenges associated with so many teenagers sleeping in a church building for a week, Urban Impact was significant for at least two reasons. First, it raised the bar in terms of public presentation. Urban Impact was very professional in appearance. The organizers gave attention to their public image and presentation through the creation of logos, stationary and arrival materials. Second, Urban Impact was significant because it was the first mission event to host evening rallies with a visiting speaker and worship leader, a development which was to be picked up again in the years ahead.

Fredericton 1992 and 1993: In early July 1993 several Fredericton, New Brunswick area churches partnered together to host Got To Be Tru. This week long program was virtually identical to another Fredericton-based youth mission project that ran the same time as Urban Impact, called Heart for the City.

Got to Be Tru involved about 120 youth from eight different churches. This event encouraged hosts and visitors to partner together in Backyard Bible Clubs that were conducted across the city of Fredericton, primarily in the subdivisions on the north side of the Saint John River. The morning clubs were followed by public ministry in the afternoon, primarily at city parks and malls. This public witness culminated with participation in the city's Canada Day parade. Some evenings and afternoons had all sorts of fun events for the students and leaders and the teams ate their suppers together in the buildings of the various churches that hosted the events.

A fireside, or vesper service, was held most evenings following the day's events. At these events students were encouraged to give testimony of how God worked through their lives during the day. They also were invited to share a verse of scripture that had become meaningful to them during the week, or even to request a song that all could sing together. Firesides proved to be a bonding time where the various groups came together as one.

Heart for the City and Got to Be Tru were important events because they demonstrated that the model developed for the event in southwestern New Brunswick was repeatable in another locale. If there had been any doubt, the Fredericton event also highlighted that ministry is more enjoyable when many people join in – the more the merrier. Youth leaders noticed positive changes in the lives of their students following the events and were convinced that there was something in this movement that was positively affecting the spiritual development of Christian teenagers.

Bold and Alive '95: Bold and Alive '95 began as an attempt by a few Moncton area churches to return the favor to the Fredericton churches that had hosted their youth groups two summers earlier. During the early meetings Bold and Alive was never viewed as a major project. At one of the early meetings one even dreamt aloud that maybe 300 people might come, but the suggestion was quickly laughed off.

By late summer 1994 a steering committee began meeting regularly and after praying about a mission statement and vision for the event, agreed on a schedule of events and sent out a letter to local churches inviting them to join in the endeavor. By Christmas 1994 over 450 teenagers and leaders had registered for the event from 37 churches, with groups coming from as far away as Maine and Ontario. The organizers were overwhelmed and in light of the unexpected large number of registrants, the entire schedule had to be reworked to accommodate the crowd.

Bold and Alive '95 introduced several new elements to the mission tour movement. It was the first event to really throw the door wide open and invite guests to come from across Canada who may not have had any previous relationship with a host church. Previous mission tour pairings were based on a preexisting relationship between host church and visiting church youth leaders. Bold and Alive '95 also introduced the concept of a closing worship rally to which adults were invited. The idea was that the profile of youth ministry would be enhanced if adults in the local area could see the quality ministry that was undertaken by the youth and the effect such involvement had upon the youth. Bold and Alive also introduced the concept of an afternoon ministry rotation. One afternoon a group would be involved in a concert of prayer, praying for the others who were out doing ministry, while another afternoon the group would be involved in a ministry of compassion such as a soup kitchen or a food drive. In the third afternoon the group was involved in a public witness ministry at a park. A final element of the 1995 event that broke new ground was the presence of a French-speaking group. This group of 10 people represented churches from across the French Baptist Union and conducted their morning and afternoon ministries in their native tongue.

While not a perfect event, Bold and Alive '95 demonstrated that the interest in mission was growing in the hearts of both youth and their leaders. Far from being a flash in the pan, the mission tour movement was here to stay.

Team Up '96: In the summer of 1994 about a dozen youth groups from Atlantic Canada travelled to Ottawa for the Canadian Baptist Federation youth conference. Many of these groups participated in mission in partnership with churches in Quebec and southern

Ontario both before and after the conference. This westward migration for mission foreshadowed an even greater westward movement that would take place in the summer of 1996.

Though it did not take place in Atlantic Canada, Team Up is an important part of the mission tour story in Atlantic Canada because nearly 300 of the 330 attendees were from New Brunswick and Nova Scotia. Team Up was held in Hamilton, Ontario and largely followed the Bold and Alive '95 model. Most of the attendees from the Maritimes were from groups that had been a part of the Moncton event one year earlier. With strong administrative support from Canadian Baptist Volunteers, the Team Up committee was chaired by Ted Durston, a layman who had been recently converted to Christ. Tragically, Durston died two years later in an automobile accident one evening following a Team Up reunion event. Dynamic worship and excellent teaching at the evening rallies capped off days that were filled with morning outreach programs for children and afternoon ministries of various sorts.

Team Up was important not only because it served to spread the experience of the mission tour movement beyond the borders of Atlantic Canada, but also because it showed that there was a loyal core of groups that were totally sold on the mission tour movement. These groups showed that they would travel over 2000 km to take part in an event that they believed would greatly benefit the spiritual lives of their teens as well as extend the influence of the gospel.

Impact '97: Impact solidified the gains made in 1995, demonstrating that the model was region-wide and not just a New Brunswick phenomenon. Impact incorporated the best of previous events and demonstrated a great deal of creativity in its programming. Taking advantage of its location, Impact provided attendees with an opportunity to tour a Navy Destroyer and watch the Nova Scotia Tattoo. The Impact committee experimented with a shortened event and sought to incorporate training as part of the week's events. A devotional guide was produced that was used by participants during the week.

Impact broke new ground in that it was the first mission tour to which churches from other denominations were welcomed as hosts and visitors, broadening the reach and influence of the movement. It also broke new ground in that it was the first event in which the host city welcomed members of its organizing committee from other centers. In fact, the chair of this Halifax event, Mike McDonald, was from Truro!

Bold and Alive '98: The schedule of Bold and Alive '98 was largely the same as the '95 project, with the incorporation of more host churches allowing the project to grow to 550 attendees. Based on their experience from 1995, the organizers made several adjustments to the program. To allow for the development of a theme, one person was asked to speak at the evening's rallies instead of a different speaker each night. Dr. Dave Currie from Abbotsford, British Columbia was well received and the experiment proved a success. Evening rallies were moved to an air-conditioned space since in previous event leaders noticed that the students and leaders needed a clear break from the summer heat. A full francophone track was added, attracting 50 teens and leaders from Quebec and New Brunswick. A website was created to provide easy access to information about the event. A team of Stewards was recruited from the Baptist Leadership Education Center in Whitby, Ontario to come and serve behind the scenes at the event. Their leadership was greatly appreciated.

Two experiments were tried which did not pan out. An "Advanced Track" was offered to students who were mission tour veterans in order to provide a higher level of challenge to some. In spite of extensive publicity including full-colour glossy brochures, it became clear that the draw of being with one's friends from one's own home church was greater than the chance to be a part of an "advanced" force. Also, a proposed "University Track", specifically targeting mission tour veterans who were too old to attend the main event, offered students an opportunity to build a house with Habitat for Humanity. This too was unsuccessful largely due to the fact that university students were either unable or unwilling to commit to an event several months in advance.

Like Bold and Alive '95, the 1998 event was filled by January demonstrating an eagerness of many groups to take part in the event. Bold and Alive '98 was critical to the development of the movement because the repeating of an event in the same area, led, at least in part, by the same people, allowed the event to be fine-tuned. Taking advantage of lessons learned from the previous event, the 1998 event had a higher level of quality and a greater influence in people's lives.

Kingdom Builders 1999: In the summer of 1999 a one-week mission project was held in Fredericton as four churches decided to host teams for a week of mission in July. Each church set and determined their own ministry projects for the week with the 10 participating teams getting together on three evenings for worship, a time of student testimonies and to hear a message from scripture.

Many of the teenagers were involved in ministry projects that were not organized in advance, but instead were created by the teenagers themselves based on the needs they saw as they walked around the city. This challenged the students not only to do ministry but also to be observant about the needs around them.

Tidal Impact 2000: The summer of 2000 saw the return of the mission tour movement to the capital of Nova Scotia. Halifax was preparing to host Assembly 2000, an event that combined the triennial meetings of Canadian Baptist Ministries, the annual Assembly of the United Baptist Convention of the Atlantic Provinces (now known as the Convention of Atlantic Baptist Churches), as well as many other gatherings.

At its first meeting in August 1999, the organizing committee decided that the youth track of Assembly 2000 should take the form of a mission tour and plans were put in place to plan an event for 425 people. With such a late start in planning, 425 was felt to be an optimistic attendance goal. It had been three years since a major mission tour had been held in the province and the local churches responded with open arms to the teenagers of Canada. Thirty-five local churches volunteered to host visiting youth teams and by January they all had visitors to host. Churches registered in droves, startling the organizers. When the dust settled, 850 teenagers from

70 churches and seven provinces showed up for an event which had to be reorganized several times to accommodate the unexpected crowd. The event became the largest youth mission project in Canadian history.

Due to the size of the event, churches from Truro, the Eastern portion of the Annapolis Valley, and the Bridgewater area were asked to host churches, creating a new situation where some teams were actually staying over two and a half hours away from other teams who attended the same event.

The event was marked by energetic evening rallies in the World Trade and Convention Center, including dynamic worship led by John Ferguson's Crave worship band and excellent messages by Dave Currie who had spoken at Bold and Alive '98. The teenagers hosted a combined total of nearly 2000 children each morning in evangelistic clubs and carried out countless ministries of compassion and public witness in the afternoons.

The closing rally, held in the Halifax Metro Center attracted nearly 2300 people, allowing the teenagers to share their worship, speaker and energy with the adults who attended. Tidal Impact 2000 was significant because it was the first mission tour that attracted interest from some churches in the African United Baptist Association.

Tidal Impact 2002: The huge interest in the 2000 mission tour suggested to the organizers that they had better pray about designing a new model to accommodate this growing event. The consensus among the strategists was that it was time to try a model that eventually was coined "One Mission: Two Cities." This model involved creating identical events in two nearby cities that shared the same budget, promotion strategy and general thrust, but for the most part operated independently during the week of the event itself. Each city had its own local planning committee and the chairs and vice chairs of each city met together periodically as a joint coordinating committee to ensure that the general thrust of the event was similar. In addition, it was the goal of the organizers for the people in the two cities to intersect two times during the week. It was planned that on one evening the youth and leaders from one city would travel to the other city for a combined rally and that on another night the opportunity would be reversed.

Moncton and Saint John were chosen as the two target cities for the New Brunswick-based event. Moncton was chosen because the Convention of Atlantic Baptist Churches had picked Atlantic Baptist University in Moncton as its location for the 2002 annual Assembly and Tidal Impact was to be the youth track for the Assembly as it had in 2000. Saint John was chosen due to its proximity to Moncton and because no major mission event has been there since 1992.

Another mission tour attendance record was set when over 1100 youth and leaders engaged in mission across southern New Brunswick from the Nova Scotia border all the way to Grand Bay-Westfield. Jim Burns from southern California spoke to the Saint John youth and Duffy Robbins from Eastern University in Pennsylvania spoke to the Moncton youth. John Ferguson's Crave led in worship in Saint John and Andrew Wigston's Present Reality led worship at the Moncton rallies. Both speakers and bands were very well received. The Moncton youth travelled to Saint John for a combined public rally on Tuesday night and a capacity crowd of over 2000 gathered for a public rally at the Lord Beaverbrook Arena. On Friday night the Saint John youth and leaders travelled to Moncton and together with the Moncton youth and leaders paraded down Killiam Drive and into the Moncton Coliseum. The adults from Convention Assembly and the many local people applauded for 20 minutes as the Tidal Impact participants marched into the rally venue, resulting in a crowd of over 3200 people – believed to be the largest crowd at a youth service in the history of New Brunswick.

The response to the event was so overwhelmingly positive that the use of two locations was adopted as the new mission tour standard.

Tidal Impact 2004: The model for the 2004 event was very much like the 2002 event. The chief difference what that for the first time since 1989 a large mission tour took place in a rural area. The churches of the upper Saint John River Valley in New Brunswick joined together to host nearly 500 visiting youth and leaders, with the evening rallies located in Florenceville's Northern Carleton

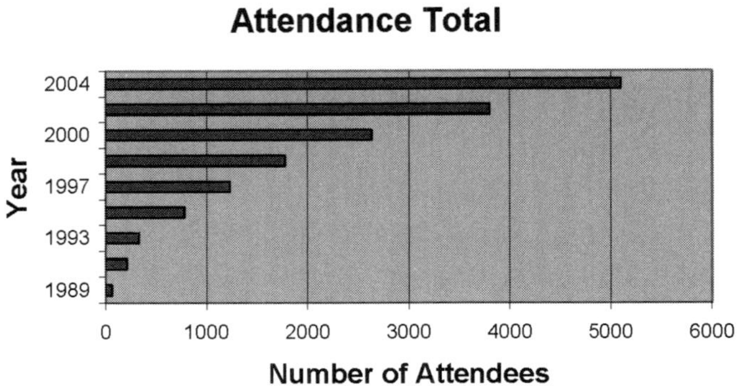

Civic Center. Together with the 800 attendees in Fredericton, the 2004 event set a new attendance record of approximately 1300 youth and leaders from 109 churches located in seven different provinces or states. Despite the growth in overall numbers, the size of the mission teams remained about the same. Though the size of the various participating teams varied quite widely, the average size of a hosting team was still 11 members and the average size of a visiting team was still 13 members. The size of participating teams was consistent with past mission tours.

By early 2004 Rob Nylen had joined the staff of the Convention's youth and family department and he and I again provided staff support to the two local committees. As in 2002 the Atlantic Baptist Youth executive took a leading role in the event and planned and led all seven afternoon concerts of prayer as well as a communion service in each city. Dave Currie returned to Tidal Impact as the speaker at the Fredericton event and Dave Overholt from the youth-targeted Church on the Rock in Hamilton, Ontario served as the speaker in Florenceville. The Jay Phillips Band led worship in Fredericton, and in Florenceville, John Ferguson's Crave led worship for an unprecedented third time.

The Tuesday night public rally in Florenceville attracted a capacity crowd of 1800 and the closing rally in Fredericton's Aitken Center attracted over 3000 guests and participants. The rallies in each location were marked by a significant moving of God's Spirit. Many of the youth made decisions to become Christian believers or to rededicate their lives the Christ. Organizers estimated conserva-

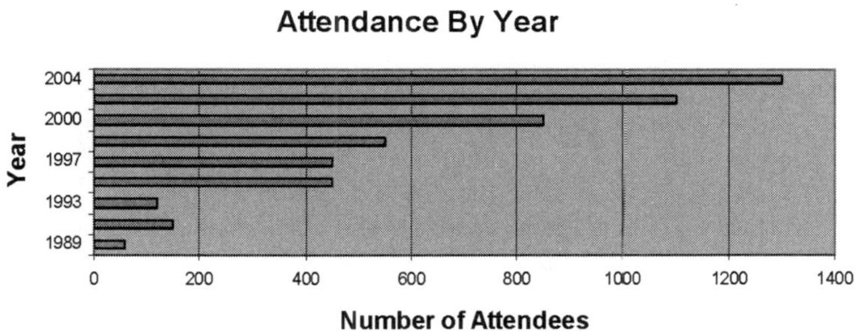

tively that as a result of morning ministries throughout the week, attendance at ministry in the parks, attendance at Sunday morning worship services and at the public rallies that the youth ministered to a total of more than 15,000 people during the week.

As in 2002 groups from across Canada attended the event, as did groups from the United States. Over ten percent of the attendees were from churches not affiliated with the Baptist Convention and several members of the planning committees came from churches that were affiliated with other denominations. A DVD of the event was produced for the first time and sent to each participant following the event.

Tidal Impact 2004 was significant for many reasons but perhaps mostly because it demonstrated that the mission tour movement need not be restricted to the small cities of Atlantic Canada. The churches of Carleton and Victoria counties in New Brunswick demonstrated that a rural area with a large enough concentration of churches can host the event with a level of quality at least equal to, if not beyond, that of a city. A key to the Florenceville experience was the role of Camp Shiktehawk. The camp cancelled its normal camping program for the week, registered all of it's staff for the event and billeted over 80 addition participants for the week. The youth based at Shiktehawk served in morning ministry in churches near the camp who were too small to billet or feed visiting youth mission teams. Although other camps had participated in previous years, no camp had ever been involved to such a significant degree.

¶ Conclusion

God shows no signs that the mission tour movement is finished. There is every indication that the past is merely prologue. The story of the mission tour movement can't help but call to mind the words of a Scott Wesley Brown song the teenagers sang at Urban Impact:

> *Look what God is doing all across the land,*
> *See his Spirit moving, feel his mighty hand....*
> *Look what God is doing, for those who do believe.*
> *Glory, Hallelujah, look what God is doing.*

Appendices

APPENDIX 1

The Discipleship Project

Job Description for Advisor

Advisor for The Discipleship Project

1. *Follow Christ.* We all make mistakes, so we don't expect you to be perfect. However, by inviting you to be an advisor we have placed a high level of trust in you and we expect you to be conscious of this fact.

2. *Pray for your student regularly.* Pray about their progress in the project and other issues in their life. Ask them what they would like you to pray about.

3. *Become familiar with the project.* Read the project description thoroughly. Become very familiar with your student's requirements.

4. *Get to know your student.* Ask them what they do for fun. Ask them about school and their family. Try to hold some of your meetings in an informal setting rather than just after church. Often much growth takes place from informal conversation and sharing.

5. *Meet with your student weekly.* Meetings normally last 15–30 minutes. During the meeting you should pray and review the memory verses learned to date. Encourage them in their ministry projects and share insights or help with questions they may have from their Bible reading.

6. *Chart their progress.* Assist your student in setting personal goals for the project and hold them accountable.

7. *Report any problems or causes for concern to the project coordinator right away.* The earlier a problem is reported, the earlier it can be dealt with. The longer you delay, the more serious the issue becomes for your student.

8. *Go the extra mile to show you care.* If time allows anything extra you can do for your student will be appreciated. A card at Christmas, a call when they are sick, spending money for the mission trip – all of these touches can be an important part of your ministry.

APPENDIX 2

The Discipleship Project

Overview & Requirements

Goal: The goal of *The Discipleship Project* is to help you become a mature disciple of Jesus Christ.

Dates: Those who have completed the trial month will be permitted to join the project when it is officially launched on November 18. The project will end on March 31.

Requirements: All participants complete the three "Common Requirements" listed below. Each participant will also be required to choose one of the options from the section entitled "Elective Requirements."

Support: To encourage and support you through the project, *The Discipleship Project* coordinator will appoint an adult advisor for each participant. Your advisor will meet with you each week to discuss with you what you have learned in your daily Bible study, to encourage you in your scripture memory, and to help you pick out ministry project options. *Arranging for meetings with your advisor is your responsibility.*

Completing this project will not be easy. The project involves a lot of work and chances are you will get discouraged at some point during the project. If you are admitted to this project, *the coordinator expects that if you get discouraged you will come and talk to him.* Many people have completed the project in the past and we know you will be able to as well.

Rewards: Those who complete *The Discipleship Project* will be invited to join:

- The church's Tidal Impact youth mission team.
- A partially subsidized fun trip to Prince Edward Island.
- A partially subsidized weekend at camp to attend Counselor-In-Training.
- A partially subsidized trip to attend the Springforth youth conference.

❡ Common Requirement 1 – Bible Reading
(*Everyone Does This*)

Goal: The goal in having you read a passage from the Bible each day is to provide you with an opportunity to learn who God is, who you are, and what God requires of you.

Requirement: You will be given a devotional guide, *Soul Journey*, which contains the reference for a Bible passage that you are to read along with a short devotional which helps you to understand the passage better. The passages and devotional must be read at least 6 days a week.

❡ Common Requirement 2 – Scripture Memory
(*Everyone Does This*)

Goal: The goal in having you acquire a basic database of scripture verses is to allow you to be used more fully by God in sharing your faith with others and helping others who are going through a difficult time. These verses will also allow you to defend your faith against those unreceptive to Christianity, and will provide you with the opportunity to concentrate and reflect upon important biblical principles.

Requirement:

a. On or before January 27, repeat Psalm 8 word for word (according to the New International Version of the Bible) for your advisor.

One week later, on or before February 3, repeat the same passage for *The Discipleship Project* coordinator.

b. On or before March 24, repeat 1 Corinthians 15:52–58 word for word (according to the New International Version of the Bible) for your advisor. One week later, on or before March 31, repeat the same passage for *The Discipleship Project* coordinator.

¶ Common Requirement 3 – Ministry Projects
(Everyone Does This)

Goal: The goal in having you participate in various ministry projects is to allow you to explore the areas the Lord has gifted you in, and to show you the joy that can come from serving others.

Requirement: Each participant must accumulate 9 ministry project points. Each project can only be done once.

Record Keeping: It is your responsibility to report to your advisor when you have completed a ministry project and how many points the project was worth. Your advisor will keep a running total of your points so that the coordinator can be advised at the conclusion of *The Discipleship Project* whether or not you have met the requirement.

Options: The following are ministry project options you may ask to participate in. The number of points the project is worth is listed beside the option, as is the name of the person whose approval you must get in order to participate in the activity. You must not accept payment for any of the projects you undertake.

Teaching:

a. Lead a devotional for a Friday evening youth group meeting.
(3 POINTS) CONTACT ____________________

Compassion:

a. Help a senior citizen with house cleaning for four hours.
(2 POINTS) CONTACT ____________________

b. Write (by post or e-mail) to a daughter or son of a missionary (at least three letters).
(3 POINTS) CONTACT ____________________

Administration:

a. Assist the church secretary with office tasks for at least two hours.
(1 POINT) CONTACT ____________________

b. Work in the church library for four Sundays.
(2 POINTS) CONTACT ____________________

c. Help organize the youth Christmas banquet.
(3 POINTS) CONTACT ____________________

d. Serve on the sanctuary pew card / pencil patrol.
(2 POINTS) CONTACT ____________________

Helping:

a. Serve in the nursery four times.
(2 POINTS) CONTACT ____________________

b. Serve as an usher in church four times
(2 POINTS) CONTACT ____________________

c. Assist with setting up, serving, and cleaning up at a church supper.
(2 POINTS) CONTACT ____________________

d. Assist with the Sunday evening children's video program for four weeks.
(2 POINTS) CONTACT ____________________

Leading:

a. Assist in a preschool or children's department Sunday School class for three weeks.
(3 POINTS) CONTACT ____________________

b. Assist in a Pioneer Club class for three weeks.
(3 POINTS) CONTACT ____________________

c. Assist with Junior Church for three weeks.
(3 POINTS) CONTACT ____________________

Maintenance:

a. Wash and clean the inside and outside of the church van.
(1 POINT) CONTACT ____________________

b. Participate in a church work night.
(2 POINTS) CONTACT ____________________

Worship Arts:

a. Sing with the youth choir in two worship services.
(2 POINTS) CONTACT ____________________

b. Read the scripture and pray in a worship service two times.
(3 POINTS) CONTACT ____________________

c. Sing a solo or sing in a small group during a worship service twice.
(2 POINTS) CONTACT ____________________

d. Play an instrument in a worship service twice.
(2 POINTS) CONTACT ____________________

Electives open only to those in High School:
(*All projects worth 9 points*)

a. Serve on the executive of *Atlantic Baptist Youth*.

b. Serve as a *The Discipleship Project* advisor to someone in grade 6 or 7.
c. Serve on the *Inter-School Christian Fellowship* executive at your school.
d. Assist with the youth Bible study program for four weeks.
e. Assist with a Pioneer Club group for 10 weeks.
f. Conduct a Bible study with a senior citizen for 10 weeks (may be done with a partner).
g. Be trained and serve as a peer counselor at the Pregnancy Resource Center.
h. Serve as a counselor or volunteer at two fall or winter retreats at camp.
i. Lead two adult mid-week services.
j. Serve as part of the Sunday morning worship band.
k. Accompany a choir regularly.
l. Produce the year in review youth group video.
m. Serve as web servant for the youth group website.

¶ Elective Requirements
(*You Choose the One You Want To Do*)

Choose one of the following options and complete it before March 31:

a. *Passage Memorization:* Memorize Colossians 1:15–20 and repeat it before your advisor and the coordinator. You may memorize from the translation of your choice.

b. *Verse Memorization:* Memorize the following 10 verses and repeat them before your advisor and the coordinator: Proverbs 28:13; 1 Peter 1:7; Ephesians 2:10; 2 Corinthians 6:14; Romans 14:10; John 5:28,29; Hebrews 9:27; Psalm 121:7,8; 1 John 5:4. You may memorize from the translation of your choice.

c. *Ministry Points:* Accumulate 8 additional ministry points.

d. *Devotional Thought:* Record in your devotional guide the answer to this question each day you read your scripture passage: "How does this passage apply to my life?" and underline in your Bible each day one new fact or truth you learned. If you are going to choose this option, you must start by week three of the project.

e. *Bible Listening:* Listen to the entire New Testament on CD. See the coordinator for the CDs. If you pick this option, don't wait until the end of the project because the CDs may not be available.

f. *Prayer For Missions:* During your quiet time each day use *Operation World* as a tool to help you pray for needs and situations around the world. See the coordinator to get a copy of *Operation World.*

g. *Potpourri:* Memorize the books of the Bible in order, find out and memorize the names of the authors of all the New Testament books, and find and memorize the shortest verse of the Bible.

h. *Research:* Choose, in consultation with the pastor, a major biblical issue you have wondered about, research the issue, and give an oral report to the pastor on the subject. You must have completed *The Discipleship Project* at least twice in order to choose this option.

i. *New Testament Reading:* Read the entire New Testament in the paraphrase or translation of your choice.

j. *Learning about Effective Missionaries:* Read two missionary biographies (life stories) and make an appointment to talk to your pastor about the books when you have finished reading them. Summarize the books for the pastor and share what you have learned. See the pastor to borrow the books.

k. *Leadership Development:* Attend two leadership development options approved by the coordinator such as: a Pioneer Clubs training event; the New Brunswick Sunday School Conference; Counselor-In-Training; Sonlife Encounter Seminar; Springforth Leaders Conference; Quest youth conference. Open only to those in grades 11 or 12.

l. *Decision Making In the Church:* Attend a meeting of the Board of Christian Education and the Board of Management, as well as the church's Annual Business Meeting with the coordinator and attend a debriefing session with him after attending all meetings. Open only to those who have completed *The Discipleship Project* two times and who are in grades 11 or 12.

m. *Educational Exploration:* Read the catalogues from three different Christian colleges or universities, meet with the coordinator and tell him: the differences between the colleges, what you like and don't like about each, and if any of the programs offered interest you. Open only to those in grades 11 or 12.

n. *Vocational Ministry:* Choose, in consultation with the pastor, three pastors to interview about their call and involvement in ministry. Ask them about: their call to ministry, their job description, their past involvement in ministry, and their preparation for ministry. Take notes from your interviews and summarize your findings in a debriefing session with the pastor. Open only to those in High School.

o. *Journal:* For a period of three months keep a spiritual journal. Entries in this may include: dialogue with a friend or relative; thoughts to yourself; a record of your dreams; lyrics to songs or poems you have written; written prayers; reflections on significant scripture verses; and reflections on the state of your spiritual journey. You should not show this journal to anyone but you do need to meet with the coordinator when you have completed this elective and tell him what you have learned from keeping a spiritual journal.

APPENDIX 3

The Discipleship Project

Trial Month

Purpose: The purpose of *The Discipleship Project* trial month is to give you the opportunity to try out some components of *The Discipleship Project* to see if you would like to join.

Dates: The trial month begins on October 28 and ends on November 18.

Who can join: Any person who regularly attends our youth group can join this project.

Requirements:

a. Using the supplied devotional guide, *Soul Journey,* read the appropriate Bible passage and the accompanying devotional at least 6 days a week.

b. Memorize the following Bible passage according to the New International Version of the Bible: Romans 5:9–11.

Conclusion: On or before November 18 each participant will meet with *The Discipleship Project* coordinator. Those who can repeat the verses listed above, word for word, and can truthfully say that they have been reading the required Bible passages and devotional thoughts will be admitted to *The Discipleship Project.*

APPENDIX 4

The Discipleship Project

Registration Form

NAME: ______________________________

ADDRESS: ______________________________

E-MAIL: ______________________________

GRADE AND SCHOOL: ______________________________

BIRTH DATE: ______________________________

PARENTS' / GUARDIANS' NAMES: ______________________________

____

I hereby indicate my desire to participate in *The Discipleship Project*. I understand that in order to be invited to participate in the promised trips and training events I need to complete the project. I also understand that it is my responsibility when I get discouraged to speak to the project coordinator.

______________________________ ______________________

SIGNATURE DATE

APPENDIX 5

The Discipleship Project

Job Description for Coordinator

1. **Refine project** (*Launch date minus eight weeks*):
   - Make any improvements to the project from the sample program contained in this book. You know your students and church; make this project fit your situation.

2. **Recruit Advisors** (*Launch date minus four weeks*):
   - Make a list of potential advisors in consultation with your pastor.
   - Mail a letter of invitation, a job description and a copy of the project.
   - Follow up the letters with a phone call.
   - Pair up the advisors with teens.
   - Have a meeting with advisors immediately before the project begins to go over their roles and answer any questions.

3. **Recruit Students** (*Launch date minus three weeks*):
   - Phone all who participated last year and invite them to participate again.
   - Make a list of new potentials in consultation with other youth leaders and call each one and invite them to participate.
   - Schedule an information session for the interested youth and give them an opportunity to sign up.

- Follow up with all who have not signed up and invite them personally.

Students begin project

4. **Review** (*Launch date plus three weeks*):
   - Call all advisors and make sure the first meeting has been held and ask them to report any difficulties immediately.
   - Call all participants and make sure they understand all that is involved in the project and answer any questions they may have. Encourage them.

5. **Reassure** (*First verse deadline minus ten days*):
   - Call all participants and remind them of the verse deadline. Find out how they are doing with the project and answer questions as necessary. Encourage them.

Students say first set of scripture verses

6. **Remind** (*End of project minus four weeks*):
   - Call all participants and find out how they are faring with the project, find out what they have left to do and encourage them.
   - Call advisors and check to see how things are going.

Students say final set of scripture verses and complete all project requirements

7. **Reward** (*End of project plus one week*):
   - Schedule a recognition moment in a morning service in consultation with the pastor.

8. **Evaluation** (*End of the project plus four weeks*):
   - Meet with students and advisors separately over dessert for feedback on the program in order to refine it for next year.

APPENDIX 6

Organizers of Large Mission Tours in Atlantic Canada

1989 Mission Tour – Southwestern New Brunswick

Mike Bravener, Union Street Baptist Church, St. Stephen, NB
John Dunnett, Lewisville Baptist Church, Moncton, NB
John Ferguson, First Baptist Church, Dartmouth, NS
Greg Pike, Marysville Baptist Church, Fredericton, NB
Jonathan Steeper, St. George Baptist Church, St. George, NB

1992 Urban Impact – Saint John, New Brunswick

John Dunnett, Kennebecasis Baptist Church, Quispamsis, NB
Roger Graham, Forest Hills Baptist Church, Saint John, NB
Scott Olsen, Kings Valley Wesleyan Church, Quispamsis, NB
Mike MacNeil, Bethany Bible College, Sussex, NB
Jerry Reddy, Main Street Baptist Church, Saint John, NB

1993 Got To Be Tru – Fredericton, New Brunswick

Phil Connor, Greenwood Drive Baptist Church, Fredericton, NB
Mike Bravener, Brunswick Street Baptist Church, Fredericton, NB
Troy Tremble, Marysville Baptist Church, Fredericton, NB

1995 Bold and Alive – Moncton, New Brunswick

Darrell Bustin, Hillside Baptist Church, Moncton, NB

Dennis Bustin, Riverview Baptist Church, Riverview, NB
Gary Dunfield, Canadian Baptist Volunteers, New Minas, NS
Bob Evans, Riverview Baptist Church, Riverview, NB
Bruce Fawcett, Lewisville Baptist Church, Moncton, NB
Heather Steeves, Canadian Baptist Volunteers, Mississauga, ON
Troy Tremble, Highfield Street Baptist Church, Moncton, NB
Paul Woodburn, Whitepine Baptist Church, Riverview, NB

1997 Impact – Halifax, Nova Scotia

Ida Armstrong-Whitehouse, Bedford Baptist Church, Bedford, NS
Gary Dunfield, Canadian Baptist Volunteers, New Minas, NS
Glenn Erskine, Immanuel Baptist Church, Truro, NS
Marlene Knowles, Windsor Baptist Church, Windsor, NS
Phil Locke, Eastern Passage Baptist Church, Eastern Passage, NS
Mike McDonald, First Baptist Church, Truro, NS
Tim McLay, New Life Baptist Church, Halifax, NS
Colin Ward, Stevens Road Baptist Church, Dartmouth, NS

1998 Bold and Alive – Moncton, New Brunswick

Scott Balser, First Baptist Church, Salisbury, NB
Dannie Brown, Atlantic Baptist University, Moncton, NB
Darrell Bustin, Hillside Baptist Church, Moncton, NB
Dennis Bustin, Atlantic Baptist University, Moncton, NB
Bruce Fawcett, Lewisville Baptist Church, Moncton, NB
John Ferguson, First Baptist Church, Moncton, NB
Perry Hanley, McKee's Mills Baptist Church, McKee's Mills, NB
Robert Landry, Eglise Baptiste Francaise de Moncton, Moncton, NB
Michael Nadeau, Canadian Baptist Volunteers, Moncton, NB
Heather Steeves, Canadian Baptist Volunteers, Mississauga, ON
Troy Tremble, Highfield Street Baptist Church, Moncton, NB
Vern Vickruck, Middle Sackville Baptist Church, Sackville, NB
Joel Wydysh, Moncton Wesleyan Church, Moncton, NB

1999 Kingdom Builders – Fredericton, New Brunswick

Gordon James, Keswick Baptist Church, Keswick, NB
Craig McCullough, Nashwaksis Baptist Church, Fredericton, NB
Mark Sypher, Brunswick Street Baptist Church, Fredericton, NB

2000 Tidal Impact – Halifax, Nova Scotia

Chris Austin, New Minas Baptist Church, New Minas, NS
Gerry & Joan Carter, Canadian Baptist Volunteers, Dartmouth, NS
Glenn Erskine, Immanuel Baptist Church, Truro, NS
Bruce Fawcett, United Baptist Convention, Moncton, NB
Rob Nylen, First Baptist Church, Dartmouth, NS
Darren Smith, West End Baptist Church, Halifax, NS
Gail Whalen-Dunn, Canadian Baptist Volunteers, Wolfville, NS

2002 Tidal Impact – Saint John & Moncton, New Brunswick

Saint John:
Bruce Fawcett, Convention of Atlantic Baptist Churches
Tim Johnson, Forest Hills Baptist Church
Jodie LeBouthillier, Grand Bay Baptist Church
Angela Marr, Germain Street Baptist Church
Lois McLean, Lancaster Baptist Church
Wayne Murphy, Norton Baptist Church
Rob Nylen, Main Street Baptist Church
Dale Stairs, Kennebecasis Baptist Church
Shawn White, Edith Avenue Baptist Church

Moncton:
Jonathan Beers, First (Salisbury) Baptist Church
Geoff Brace, Camp Wildwood
Darrell Bustin, Hillside Baptist Church
Bruce Fawcett, Convention of Atlantic Baptist Churches
John Ferguson, Allison Baptist Church
Robert Landry, Eglise Baptiste Francaise de Moncton
Phil MacCormack, First (Hillsborough) Baptist Church

Darren McHarg, Lewisville Baptist Church
Chet McPhail, Dundas Baptist Church
Claire Peveril, Middle Sackville Baptist Church
Tim Richardson, Lewisville Baptist Church
Jillian Somers, Atlantic Baptist Youth
Phil Woodworth, Sussex Baptist Church

Coordinating Committee:
Rob Nylen, Chair, Saint John
Dale Stairs, Vice Chair, Saint John
Darrell Bustin, Chair, Moncton
Darren McHarg, Vice Chair, Moncton
Gerry and Joan Carter, Registrars
Bruce Fawcett, Director

2004 Tidal Impact – Florenceville and Fredericton, New Brunswick

Fredericton:
Mark Archibald, Nashwaaksis Baptist Church
Sandi Braun, St. Paul's United Church
Joe Crummey, The Meeting Place
David Egers, Greenwood Drive Baptist Church
Bruce Fawcett, Convention of Atlantic Baptist Churches
Bonnie Hunt, Christ Church Parish
Mark Hunter, Douglas Baptist Church
Cindy Keizer, Smythe Street Cathedral
Chris Price, Marysville Baptist Church
Mark Sypher, Brunswick Street Baptist Church
Joel Wydysh, Corbett Avenue Wesleyan Church

Florenceville:
Andrea Baird, Inter-Varsity Christian Fellowship
Stephen Budd, Tracey Mills Baptist Church
Stephen Cogswell, Woodstock Baptist Church
Kelly Cogswell, Woodstock Baptist Church
Dan Jamer, Hartland Baptist Church

Marion Jamer, Hartland Baptist Church
Andrew Matthews, Perth-Andover Baptist Church
Kevin Myers, Hartland Wesleyan Church
Rob Nylen, Convention of Atlantic Baptist Churches
Mike Palmer, Aroostook Baptist Church
Rene Robichaud, Shiktehawk Bible Camp
Valerie Slipp, Grafton Baptist Church
Ben Trites, Jacksonville Baptist Church
Ian Tupper, Coldstream Baptist Church

Coordinating Committee:
Andrea Baird, Chair, Florenceville
Ben Trites, Vice Chair, Florenceville
Mark Sypher, Chair, Fredericton
Joel Wydysh, Vice Chair, Fredericton
Gerry Carter, Registrar
Rob Nylen, Director
Bruce Fawcett, Director

APPENDIX 7

Sample Schedule

Tidal Impact 2004, Florenceville, NB

	SAT 31st	SUN 1st	MON 2nd	TUES 3rd	WED 4th	THUR 5th	FRI 6th
MORN		Worship with Host Church	Morning ministry / prep and promo	Ministry with partner church	Ministry with partner church	Ministry with partner church	Ministry with partner church
AFT	Arrival supper with host church	Ministry preparation for the next day	New Brunswick Day Ministry ADC Group Supper 5:00	Group A Park Ministry	Group A Ministry Electives	Group A Fun Event 2–4:30 ABU Group Supper 5:00	Group A Concert of Prayer 2–4:15
EVEN	Community building with partner church	Evening Rally 6:30–8:30 Register during rally	Evening Rally 6:30–8:30	Joint Public Rally in Flo'ville 7:00–9:00	Fun event with host church	Evening Rally with Communion Service 6:30–9:00	Joint Public Rally F'ton 7:00–9:00

APPENDIX 8

Sample Registration Form

The following is sample text for a registration form taken from the forms used for Springforth 2004 (Gros Morne/Twin Ponds, Newfoundland, May 19–24, 2004) and Tidal Impact 2004 (Fredericton/Florenceville, NB, July 31– Aug. 6, 2004).

Springforth 2004 - Gros Morne/Twin Ponds, Newfoundland (May 19th - 24th, 2004)
Tidal Impact 2004 - Fredericton/Florenceville, N.B. (July 31st - Aug. 6th, 2004)

Mission Tour Registration Form

Please return this form, completed in full, with initial deposits for either/both events.
22 Seats are available on a first-come-first-served basis.

Name:______________________________ ______________ ______________
Family Name/Last Name/Surname **First Name** **Middle Name(s)**

Date of Birth:________________ **Age on May 19th, 2004:**______**years old**
Month Day Year

Address:____
Street/Mailing Address

______________ ______________ ___ ___ ___ - ___ ___ ___
Town/City **Province** **Postal Code**

Phone: (Home)______________ **(Work)**______________ **(Emergency)**______________

Personal E-mail Address of Team Member: ______________________________

Provincial Health Plan Number: ___ ___ ___ ___ ___ ___ ___ ___ ___

Additional Health Coverage:______________________ ______________________
(Carrier: ie. Blue Cross, Aetna) **Plan Number**

T-shirt size (circle one): Small Medium Large Extra-large

I hereby indicate my plans to participate in the Mission Tour(s) of Hanwell Community Church, in 2004 (check which ones apply):

Springforth, Newfoundland - Wed., May 19th to Mon., May 24th, 2004	❑	$300.00
Tidal Impact 2004 - Sat., July 31st to Fri., Aug. 6th, 2004	❑	$109.00
		$409.00

I promise to follow the program completely and to abide by the rules set down by my pastor/leaders. I understand that the approximate cost to me for the Newfoundland trip is $300.00, that the Tidal Impact event in Fredericton is $109.00, and that my initial deposit for either of these trips is a non-refundable payment towards securing my placement. Also, I understand that if I opt out of this project at a later date that I might possibly forfeit all or part of my fees, if another person is not found to take my place.
The amounts are due as follows:

$50.00 Initial Deposit for Newfoundland	- due by December 10th, 2003.
$60.00 Initial Deposit for Tidal Impact	- due by January 28th, 2004.
$75.00 Second Deposit for Newfoundland	- due by February 25th, 2004.
$75.00 Third Deposit for Newfoundland	- due by March 31st, 2004.
$100.00 Balance for Newfoundland	- due by May 5th, 2004.
$49.00 Balance for Tidal Impact	- due by June 2nd, 2004.

All balances may be reduced by fund raising, however, raised funds are non-refundable. Preferable to cash, all deposits should be cheques or money orders made payable to: "Hanwell Community Church," and remitted to the pastor, Rev. Mike McDonald. All amounts qualify for receipts for income tax purposes, as this is a "Missions" project.

______________________________ ______________
Signature of Participant/Youth Group Member **Date (Month/Day/Year)**

MEDICAL HISTORY

Date of last tetanus shot (if known, otherwise mark "unknown"):_________________________

Please indicate with a check mark if you have a history of any of the following:
__Diabetes __Asthma __Epilepsy __Kidney __Heart Disease __Allergies

If any of the above are checked, please elaborate on medical details below.

Other Medical Information (attach an additional sheet if necessary):

____

____

____

Is there any additional information regarding restrictions (ie. diet, physical activities, etc.)?

____

Family Doctor:____
Name Address Phone Number

Emergency Number to reach next of kin/a family member during May 19th - 24th, 2004:

____

Number	Location (ie. Home/Work)	Name of Contact	Relationship (ie. Parent/Friend)

***** NOTE: Parent/Legal Guardian to sign only if participant is under the age of 19 *****

I hereby give permission for my son/daughter to participate in Springforth, Newfoundland from May 19th to 24th, 2004 and/or Tidal Impact: Ride the Wave, Fredericton/Florenceville, New Brunswick, July 31st to August 6th, 2004, the Mission Tours for Hanwell Community Church. In case of emergency, I hereby give permission to the physician selected by my son/daughter's pastor/leaders to hospitalize, secure proper treatment for, and to order injection, anesthesia or surgery for my child as named on this form. I also realize that it is my responsibility to obtain proper health insurance coverage for my child during this time.

______________________________ ______________________

Signature of Parent/Legal Guardian **Date (Month/Day/Year)**

______________________________ ______________________

Please PRINT Name of Parent/Legal Guardian **Parent(s)' E-mail Address**

Youth and Family Ministries

The youth and family ministry department of the Convention was established in 2001 to nurture and support healthy ministries to youth and families by churches across the Convention. This ministry continues and builds upon the Convention's long-term youth ministry emphasis. Currently, the churches of the Convention minister weekly to over 5000 teenagers and many churches are developing ministries in support of the family.

Some of the events and initiatives sponsored by the department include the following (extensive information is available at *www.baptist-atlantic.ca*):

Events for Youth, ages 12–18

Springforth: An annual spring youth conference attended by over 2000 youth and leaders.

Tidal Impact: A biennial summer mission experience that has grown to become Canada's largest youth mission program.

High School Quest: A biennial summer leadership conference that is sponsored by Atlantic Baptist Youth and held during Convention Assembly.

Middle School Quest: A biennial summer conference for Middle School / Junior High students which equips them to share their faith effectively with their peers; held during Convention Assembly.

Equipping and Encouragement for Youth Leaders

Sonlife Encounter Seminar: A one-day introductory seminar held each fall for new youth leaders. Jointly sponsored with Atlantic Baptist University.

Springforth Leaders Conference: An annual conference for volunteer leaders held during the Springforth youth conference.

Youth Pastors' Summit: A two-day gathering for youth pastors and spouses for networking, fun and personal growth.

National Youthworkers Conference: A biennial fall national conference for paid and volunteer youth leaders for rest, fun, and personal renewal. Jointly sponsored with Canadian Baptist Ministries.

ADC/ABU Youth Ministry Intersession: A one-week youth ministry course offered each January. Jointly sponsored with Atlantic Baptist University and Acadia Divinity College.

Acadia Youth Ministry Institute: An annual one-week youth ministry course, sometimes offered overseas. Sponsored jointly with Acadia Divinity College.

Mutual Mentoring Mission Trips: Periodic overseas mission experiences for veteran youth pastors from across Canada. Sponsored jointly with Canadian Baptist Ministries.

Speaking: Both the Associate Director and Director speak regularly at churches, conferences, camps and youth events to provide customized training and encouragement.

Young Adults

Atlantic Baptist Youth: An opportunity for young adults to be elected to serve on an executive which provides leadership for youth and young adult events.

Leadership Exchange: Providing opportunities for young adults from Atlantic Canada to participate in the leadership of major Baptist youth events in other parts of Canada. Sponsored jointly with Canadian Baptist Ministries.

Short-term Mission: An annual two-week overseas mission opportunity for young adults from across Canada. Sponsored jointly with Canadian Baptist Ministries.

Converge Young Adult Worship Festival: An annual young adult worship festival sponsored by Atlantic Baptist Youth and Intervarsity Christian Fellowship.

Family Ministry

Family Mission Tour: A one-week mission experience for families, held in Atlantic Canada.

Mission: Possible parenting conference: An annual travelling series of one evening parenting conferences for parents of teens and preteens as well as pastors and youth leaders.

Link: Clergy Teen Escape Weekend: An annual retreat for the teenage children of pastors and other Christian workers.

Ministry Wives Retreat: An annual weekend retreat planned and led by ministry wives for ministry wives.

Leadership for these initiatives is provided by the staff of the department and by dozens of youth leaders, youth pastors, and others who serve on a variety of working groups and teams that plan and lead various events.

Through you and your church's generous giving to the Convention's United in Mission fund you are supporting these vital ministries which provide support and encouragement to our churches as they seek to reach and minister to youth and families.

About the Authors

Rev. Bruce Fawcett

A native of Moncton, New Brunswick, Bruce is Director of Youth and Family Ministries for the Convention of Atlantic Baptist Churches (*www.baptist-atlantic.ca*). Prior to that, he served as Associate Pastor for Youth at the Lewisville Baptist Church in Moncton, New Brunswick. He also taught Youth Leadership, Greek, and Religious Studies at Atlantic Baptist University (*www.abu.nb.ca*). Currently, he teaches at Acadia Divinity College (*http://adc.acadiau.ca*) in Wolfville, Nova Scotia, where he is Director of the Youth Ministry Program, lecturing in the areas of youth ministry, leadership, and mission.

A graduate of Atlantic Baptist University (B.A.), Gordon-Conwell Theological Seminary (M.Div.), and Harvard University (Th.M.), Bruce is currently completing a Ph.D. at the University of Wales in the United Kingdom. Bruce speaks frequently on the subject of youth ministry at conferences, churches, and camps and has been a visiting instructor at colleges and seminaries in Canada, the United States, and overseas. He and his wife Penny and their two children, Daniel and Emily, make their home near Saint John, New Brunswick.

Rev. Mike McDonald

Born into an air force family in Winnipeg, Manitoba, Mike has lived across Canada and overseas. He is currently serving as Senior Pastor of Hanwell Community Church: Convention of Atlantic Baptist Churches, Inc. (*http://personal.nbnet.nb.ca/hanwellc*), a relatively new church plant on the outskirts of Fredericton, New Brunswick. Mike has been involved in youth ministry throughout Atlantic Canada, particularly by taking youth groups from Nova

Scotia, Prince Edward Island and New Brunswick on mission tours to Newfoundland. Coming into his 20th year of youth ministry, Mike served as a volunteer at First Baptist Church, Dartmouth, a seminary student at Wolfville Baptist Church, Wolfville, Nova Scotia, as Associate Pastor for over seven years at First Baptist Church, Truro, Nova Scotia, and as a Youth Pastor at both First Baptist Church, Charlottetown and Cornerstone Baptist Church, Cornwall, both on Prince Edward Island.

A graduate of Loyalist College of Applied Arts & Technology (Diploma of Business Administration), Belleville, Ontario, Mike also graduated from both Acadia University (B.B.A.) and Acadia Divinity College (M.Div.) in Wolfville, Nova Scotia. He has taken part in 18 mission tours since 1988, and was chair of the first "Impact" national mission tour project in Halifax in 1997. Mike was engaged to his wife Angela, just prior to his first mission tour, and his oldest child just completed her first mission tour. They live near the church in Hanwell with their three children, Kathleen, Sarah and Allan.

Rev. Rob Nylen

Rob Nylen is from Saskatoon, Saskatchewan, and is currently serving as Associate Director in the Youth and Family Ministry Department for the Convention of Atlantic Baptist Churches. Previously, Rob was the Associate Pastor at Main Street Baptist Church in Saint John, New Brunswick. He has also served at First Baptist Church in Dartmouth, Nova Scotia, Chester Baptist Church in Nova Scotia and Highfield Baptist Church in Moncton, New Brunswick.

Rob has served on the Executive Committee for Tidal Impact 2000 in Halifax, 2002 in Moncton/Saint John, and 2004 in Fredericton/Florenceville. Rob currently teaches at Acadia Divinity College in the Youth Ministry Program.

Rob is a graduate of Atlantic Baptist University (B.A. Sociology) and Acadia Divinity College (M.Div.). He and his wife Jill have three children, Nicholas, Ethan and Annaliese.